Bulletin 392
Development Policy & Practice

Natural Resource Management in West Africa
Towards a knowledge management strategy

Floris van der Pol and Suzanne Nederlof (eds)

Table of contents

Acronyms and abbreviations   5
Acknowledgements   7
Introduction   8

1   **Knowledge management for development: setting the scene**   10
Sarah Cummings and Floris van der Pol
Introduction   10
1.1   What is knowledge management?   11
1.2   Tools and techniques   12
1.3   Knowledge management in natural resource management   13
1.4   Examples of knowledge management for specific subjects in NRM   14
1.5   Examples of knowledge management at various levels   16
1.6   The home-grown approach   18

2   **Knowledge management on soil and water conservation in southern Mali**   20
Floris van der Pol, Ferko Bodnár and Zana Sanogo
Introduction   20
2.1   Introducing soil and water conservation in the cotton-growing area of Mali   20
2.2   Knowledge on soil and water conservation in southern Mali, its content and origin   21
2.3   Whose knowledge?   23
2.4   Knowledge management activities   24
2.5   Strategic knowledge management aspects   26
2.6   Conclusions   30

3   **Farmer-managed natural regeneration in Niger: a case study in knowledge management**   31
Chris Reij, Mahamane Larwanou, Adam Toudou and Yamba Boubabcar
Introduction   31
3.1   Re-greening the Sahel   32
3.2   Where knowledge goes   35
3.3   The impact of knowledge on farmer-managed natural regeneration   39
3.4   Conclusions   40

4	Knowledge management in the Integrated Soil fertility Management Project in Togo	41

Constant Dangbégnon, Suzanne Nederlof, Adonko Tamelokpo and Abdoulaye Mando

	Introduction	41
4.1	Introducing adapted fertilization practices in Togo	41
4.2	Knowledge content: how to maintain soil fertility under more intensive cultivation	43
4.3	Whose knowledge?	46
4.4	Knowledge management activities	47
4.5	Towards a KM approach: creating knowledge impact	50
4.6	Conclusions	55

5	Knowledge management for introducing soil and water conservation into the agricultural practices of the Mahi people in Benin	56

Constant Dangbégnon, Suzanne Nederlof, Mathias Ahounou and Gustave Kpagbin

	Introduction	56
5.1	From shifting cultivation to more permanent agriculture in Benin	56
5.2	Knowledge content: soil and water conservation in Ouèsse	58
5.3	Whose knowledge?	61
5.4	Knowledge management activities	63
5.5	Towards a KM approach: creating knowledge impact	65
5.6	Conclusions	69

6	Knowledge management on natural resources in West Africa: Towards a strategy?	70

Suzanne Nederlof and Floris van der Pol

6.1	Knowledge management in the four cases revisited	70
6.2	The knowledge managers and the process	72
6.3	Coming to a knowledge management strategy	75

References	78
About the authors	85

Acronyms and abbreviations

AAR	After Action Review
ADB	Asian Development Bank
CGICE	Centre for Information and Knowledge Management on the Environment
CIDA	Canadian International Development Agency
CILSS	Inter-State Agency for Drought Control in the Sahel
CIS	Center for International Cooperation of VU University of Amsterdam
CoPs	communities of practice
CRESA	Centre Régional pour l'Enseigment Supérieur en Agriculture
DFID	Department for International Development, UK
FAO	Food and Agriculture Organization
FARA	Forum for Agricultural Research in Africa
GEF	Global Environment Fund
GTZ	German Technical Development
ICTs	information and communication technologies
IFAD	International Fund for Agricultural Development
IFC	International Finance Corporation
IKM	information and knowledge management
ILO	International Labour Organization
IRC	International Resources Group (Washington, DC)
ISRIC	International Soil Reference and Information Centre
IT	information technology
KfD	Knowledge for Development, USAID
KM	knowledge management
KM4D	knowledge management for development
KS	knowledge sharing
MDGs	Millennium Development Goals
NARS	National Agricultural Research Institutes
NEPAD	New Partnership for Africa's Development
NGOs	non-governmental organizations
PRSA	Projet de Restructuration des Services Agricoles
PSA	Public Service Agreement
RAAKS	Rapid Appraisal of Rural Agricultural Knowledge System
SDA	Service Delivery Agreement
SDC	Swiss Agency for Development and Cooperation
SFI	Soil Fertility Initiative
Sida	Swedish International Development Agency
SSA	Sub-Saharan Africa

TRIZ	Theory of innovative problem solving
WHO	World Health Organization
WISP	World Initiative on Sustainable Pastoralism
WOCAT	World Overview of Conservation Approaches and Technologies
UN	United Nations
UNDP	United Nations Development Programme
UNFCCC	United Nations Climate Change Convention
USGS	United States Geological Survey
USAID	US Agency for International Development

Acknowledgements

The Royal Tropical Institute has developed this bulletin on the basis of lessons learned in Western Africa. The documentation process, of which this bulletin is a final product, was only possible through the financial assistance of the Dutch Ministry of Foreign Affairs and the time and other resources contributed by associates in Western Africa as well as at the Royal Tropical Institute in Amsterdam.

This publication was developed on the basis of a number of case studies in Mali, Niger, Benin and Togo, which were documented by authors working in the respective countries. These authors are:
Mali   Floris van der Pol, Ferko Bodnár and Zana Sanogo;
Niger   Chris Reij, Mahamane Larwanou, Adam Toudou and Yamba Boubabcar;
Togo   Constant Dangbégnon, Suzanne Nederlof, Adonko Tamelokpo and Abdoulaye Mando;
Benin   Constant Dangbégnon, Suzanne Nederlof, Mathias Ahounou and Gustave Kpagbin.

Case studies could only be documented thanks to contributions by many other stakeholders in the respective countries, who participated bilaterally with the referred authors.

This bulletin was peer reviewed by (and greatly benefited from the comments of) Sarah Cummings of Context, international cooperation, Utrecht, and Paul Engel of the European Centre for Development Policy Management, Maastricht. We thank Kimberly Clarke for the language editing.

Floris van der Pol
Suzanne Nederlof

Introduction

Ensuring environmental sustainability in rural areas and reversing the loss of environmental resources is key to eradicating poverty and hunger. Numerous recent documents and initiatives recognize this need – including from the New Partnership for Africa's Development (NEPAD), World Bank (TerrAfrica) and the Forum for Agricultural Research in Africa (FARA) – and stress the importance of renewed attention for sustainable agricultural production and natural resource management.

Studies indicate that the poor are often disproportionately affected by environmental degradation, from health risks, loss of livelihoods, and natural and man-made disasters. The poor also have limited options to mitigate or avoid the consequences of this degradation. Often, environmental degradation and loss of livelihoods are the origin of conflicts and destabilizing migratory movements.

Especially in West Africa, with its ongoing processes of democratic decentralization and privatization, more and more actors are expected to play their role in sustainable resource management in rural areas, and they have an obvious need for information. Simultaneously, as a result of the decrease in funding for rural programmes, existing knowledge and experiences are scattered and disappearing. There is a great risk of losing the benefits of the millions invested in land resource management between 1990 and 2000.

Society's learning capacity in the field of sustainable land resource management is at stake and more emphasis on knowledge management is needed to guarantee that the accumulated knowledge is shared in such a way that the right actors have appropriate knowledge at the right time to take the best decisions. Efficient policies governing structures for national and regional knowledge management need to be formulated and the working procedures of the various actors in the field need to be defined more sharply.

The question is, how can this be achieved in the current situation in West Africa, with its multitude of actors working in rural development? This book aims to help find answers to this question. For that purpose four groups active in managing knowledge on land resources in West Africa have been asked to write up their personal experiences and reflect on how they see their 'knowledge management' activities (even if they did not call them that at the time). Based on these contributions we discuss the question of 'how we can build a knowledge management strategy in the region'?

This Bulletin starts with a short presentation to set the scene. What is knowledge management? What tools are used? What are the main activities in the field of natural resource management? Subsequently four case studies are presented to illustrate the broader context of knowledge management on land resources in the region. Finally, we draw lessons from these case studies.

1 Knowledge management for development: setting the scene

Sarah Cummings and Floris van der Pol

Introduction

Since the mid-1990s the importance of knowledge for development has been increasingly acknowledged, illustrated by a quote from the World Bank (see Box 1). Knowledge management (KM), which originated in management science, has been applied in commercial organizations and has been partially accepted by the development establishment. In its original sense, it referred to managerial support for learning within and between organizations, and consequently the effective use of knowledge. In the economy of knowledge management theories the value of knowledge is expressed in terms of economic, social and ecological value. In the first wave of knowledge management for development, up to 2000, the leading organizations were the World Bank, the British Department for International Development (DFID) and the United Nations Development Programme (UNDP), where the 'stealth' approach based on communities of practice (CoPs) was later mainstreamed through a 'big bang' approach in thematic networks and regional centres (Henderson 2005). Knowledge management has come and gone among some of the leaders, 'most notably the World Bank where their pioneering knowledge sharing programme seems to have all but disappeared'.

> **Box 1   Importance of knowledge**
>
> International institutions, country donors and the broader development community are rapidly coming to the conclusion that knowledge is central to development – that knowledge is development.
> World Bank, 1998.

Since then, many factors have transformed the way organizations view knowledge and knowledge sharing. But perhaps the most pivotal is the dramatically extended reach of knowledge through new information and communication technologies (ICTs), and particularly the Internet. Barnard and colleagues (2006) argue that this caused a second wave of knowledge management initiatives in development. Many others followed, including the international research organizations. Pineiro (2005) considers some of the major trends in agricultural science and technology and the role of CGIAR centres. He sees a particular challenge in

> **Box 2   Importance of knowledge management**
>
> …No one should be dying or suffering because knowledge that already exists in one part of the world has not reached other parts. It is up to each of us to take the responsibility to ensure the knowledge flows easily to where it is needed.
> Foreword by Geoff Parcell in Ramalingam, 2006: p. 1.

developing institutional and policy frameworks that promote knowledge management processes.

The diverse efforts of organizations around the world are being pursued under various labels: knowledge management, knowledge sharing, intellectual capital management and intellectual asset management. In a complex sense, knowledge management is four things at the same time: it is a concept, a business discipline or theory that reflects the increasing importance of knowledge as a corporate asset, a collection of technologies, and a philosophy. Many of the varied definitions focus on one or more of these aspects.

Knowledge management originated as an in-company strategy. It offered a new window to development organizations, especially because development activities themselves comprise knowledge-based practices. Today, with liberalization and decentralization, more emphasis is put on development as a multi-actor process with responsibilities at different levels. How to organize knowledge management in such a context is a question that has yet to be answered.

The following three sections describe briefly some of the main themes in knowledge management.

1.1 What is knowledge management?

Knowledge management is an interdisciplinary field with its roots in business management, psychology, librarianship, and information science and technology. Its focus is on knowledge as a resource. Practitioners summarize, contextualize, value-judge, rank, synthesize and edit to make information and knowledge accessible to a target audience, either within or outside of their organization. Fundamental concepts include social learning, organizational learning, and best practics, largely based on tacit interpretation and less on rules. In this view local knowledge is also a knowledge management subject, with the local population as the above-mentioned practitioners. Networks, online communities, yellow pages, intranets and extranets, and websites are generally the focus of knowledge-management activities.

In a development context, knowledge management aims to facilitate exchange and cross-fertilization by providing access to knowledge both within and outside of the organization, accumulating knowledge from various organizations. It is sometimes used interchangeably with "knowledge sharing". In this context the distinction is emphasized between so-called 'tacit' or 'informal' knowledge and more 'explicit' or 'formal' knowledge (see Box 3). Joint learning with farmers and introducing local farmers to scientific knowledge may lead to the **social construction of new knowledge**. Subsequently, the new knowledge should be shared with a larger population, scaling up the knowledge management.

Pels and Odhiambo (2005), in their Learn@WELL knowledge-management module, distinguish three levels of knowledge management: (1) the personal level; (2) the organizational level; and (3) the multi-stakeholder network level. Geographic scales have also been defined. In general there is a relationship between the geographic scale of KM activities and the degree of specialization of the content: at global level KM activities

> **Box 3   Types of knowledge**
>
> *Implicit and explicit knowledge*
> Implicit knowledge is considered to be the knowledge we have that has not been expressed as such. It is not associated with a body of formal written information concerning the knowledge. The opposite of this is explicit knowledge, which is accessible through a variety of media channels.
>
> *Tacit and conscious knowledge*
> The term tacit knowledge originates with Polanyi (1958), and has been described as: "the idea that certain cognitive processes and/or behaviors are undergirded by operations inaccessible to consciousness" (Barbiero, n.d.), both cited in Wilson (2002). In this way tacit knowledge is hidden knowledge, hidden even from the consciousness of the knower, as is reflected by Polanyi using the phrase "We know more than we can tell". The opposite of this is conscious knowledge, knowledge that we are aware of and that we could eventually communicate.
>
> In this bulletin we will follow current practice and use the term '*tacit*' knowledge as implicit knowledge.

pertain to specific subjects such as soil conservation technology or soil erosion (for example www.wocat.net, www.soilerosion.net), or value-chain development (see for example Elias et al (2006) on knowledge sharing in the African shea sector), while at village level KM activities pertain to the more general information on health, livelihood, food, water, and income security (see Village Knowledge centres, www.thehindu.com/2005/11/25/stories/2005112504941000).

1.2   Tools and techniques

A variety of technical tools are employed for development knowledge management (see Box 4). There does not appear to be any systematic comparison of which of these tools are the most successful – they are applied to reach different strategic objectives.

For example, the experience with CoPs and knowledge networks generally seems to have been successful in linking professional expertise and practices. Clark (2006) focuses on the visual impact of network maps as perceived by local stakeholders in value chains in Bolivia. They discuss how network mapping can help actors understand their local networks and develop their own skills to both analyse and strengthen these networks in order to support improved planning and implementation of local development initiatives. Douthwaite et al. (2006) analyse the function of networks in strengthening rural groups in Colombia. Mchombu (2003) and later Matovelo et al. (2005) analyse the importance of information dissemination for development in Tanzania: almost all questioned farmers expressed a desire for information about different agricultural innovations for improving agricultural practices. The professional's role could be to find mechanisms that would empower farmers to become proactive in acquiring information, for example by using recorded sources of information rather than remaining passive recipients of information. Lightfoot and Scheuermeier (2006) describe building knowledge management strategies for effective rural development in East Africa (Linking Local Learners). They conclude that encouraging local actors to exchange experiences using modern ICTs could eventually become sustainable if (1) the level of awareness of the general population of the potential benefits is raised and (2) if there is sufficient reliable and relevant local content. They see considerable potential for the integration of market and ICT services.

> **Box 4   Knowledge management tools in development**
>
> - communities of practice (CoPs) and knowledge networks
> - field days/exchange visits
> - Farmer Field Schools
> - 'how to' guides
> - interdisciplinary seminars, discussion groups
> - virtual team working and web casts
> - intranet
> - daily organizational newspapers
> - programme assessment systems
> - databases
> - e-mail
> - document and record management systems
> - mapping of competency needs
> - facilitation training for managers, team-working, mentoring and e-learning
> - yellow pages (inventories of expertise and contact details)

Other tools that emerged are blogs, podcasting, RSS, wikis and many more. In terms of techniques, Peer Assists and After Action Reviews were the most widely documented. Story telling is also popular. For an overview of tools and techniques, Ramalingam (2006) is highly recommended.

1.3   Knowledge management in natural resource management

'Natural resource management' (NRM) involves the use and management of land, water, forest and biological resources, and it is fundamentally related to people and their livelihoods. NRM presents a clear need for knowledge management among and between farmers and NRM practitioners with various backgrounds and interests and from various organizations and countries.

There has been very little formal knowledge management applied to knowledge systems in developing countries themselves, and certainly not to NRM in this context. Most KM was applied to organizations internally, and also to the establishment of global knowledge-sharing mechanisms (such as the World Bank's Development Gateway). The work of Engel and Solomon (1997) and related work is of interest for NRM, as it is the emerging approach developed by researchers at the CGIAR centres which links Engel's home-grown approach with that of the broader knowledge management for development (KM4D) approach (see eg Douthwaite 2006/7). The growing interest in KM by the NRM sector is also demonstrated by the KM profile of the FAO (FAO, 2006).

Related KM activities in the field of water and sanitation have been described by Pels and Odhiambo (2005) (a Learn@WELL knowledge management module) and by Visscher et al. (2006) (a thematic overview of knowledge and information management in the water and sanitation sector). Bhowmik (2006) applied the TRIZ (Theory of inventive problem solving) framework – which is based on using knowledge from comparable cases (see Figure 1) – to global problems of environmental pollution.

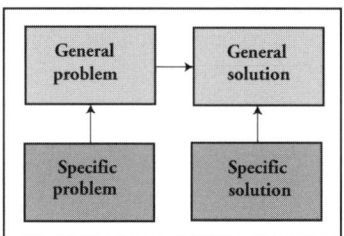

Figure 1 The TRIZ framework: Using general knowledge to solve specific problems

1.4 Examples of knowledge management for specific subjects in NRM

Knowledge management is frequently organized by subject. KM activities on some main subjects in Natural Resource Management are presented below.

Forestry

Buchholz (2005) analysed information and knowledge management (IKM) systems for forestry and NRM in South-East Asia. German Technical Development (GTZ) has been supporting the NRM sector in this area for nearly 30 years. Although much of the knowledge gained has been documented within the projects, a systematic and comprehensive assessment, analysis and documentation of the entire knowledge base has not been undertaken. The author concludes that access to the lessons learned and knowledge of these projects is limited.

The proceedings of a Global Environmental Fund (GEF) Forum in 2006 describe the application of KM to forest resources, land management and pastoralism (Davies, 2006). For sustainable forest management the approach had two steps:
- **Indicator development**: A range of indicators has been developed (252 indicators of change) and progress towards SFM has been assessed.
- **Bringing together information**: Information has been compiled for 229 countries and territories, with the participation of more than 800 specialists from all over the world.

Indicator development took a large part of the work.

Sustainable Land Management, soil conservation and soil fertility

For sustainable land management the GEF Forum in 2006 gave an approach comprising three activities:
- **Indicator development**: Develop indicators for the benefits of combating land degradation.
- **Knowledge exchange:** Exchange and disseminate knowledge and experiences through a Learning Network.

- **Impact measurement**: Measure impacts through a harmonized GEF-inter-agency monitoring and evaluation approach.

Liniger et al. (2002) documented experiences of the 'World Overview of Conservation Approaches and Technologies' (WOCAT) tools in local, national and global programmes. WOCAT was initiated as early as 1992. They conclude that the great challenge is to prove that information can be used for better land management at lower implementation levels.

The IIED series Managing Africa's Soils[1] covers meso-level cases of soil fertility management. IFDC (the International Center for Soil Fertility and Agriculture Development), through its well-known *IFDC Reports* series, but also though organizing and participating in knowledge exchange at various levels, contributes to the development of a body of knowledge on soil fertility management and the use of various types of fertilizers.

Soil nutrient balances have been used to communicate and generate knowledge on the evolution of soil fertility over time (FAO, 2004). Van der Pol and Moukoko (1992) and FAO (2005) gave soil nutrient flows an economic value to compare the value of depleted nutrients with those of the crops produced. Knowledge from various disciplines (water/civil engineers, agronomists, crop specialists, mineralogists, economists) is brought together for such an assessment.

Pastoralism

The World Initiative on Sustainable Pastoralism (WISP) presented its KM approach at the GEF forum:
- **Gather existing knowledge** from pastoralists, secondary data and experts.
- **Develop knowledge** by linking the skills of pastoralists with researchers and cross-country learning.
- **Promote the use of knowledge bases** (websites, publications, CD-ROMs, mapping, translation, repackaging for different audiences).
- **Distribute knowledge** through publications, presentations, cross-country exchanges, and by empowering pastoralists (presentations to gatherings).
- **Apply the knowledge**: Policy dialogue (government, UN, global processes, donors, NGOs, pastoralists, media, private sector), learning recommendations.

The programme aimed to generate impact by influencing global processes (presentations in UN meetings), opinions (organizing global and regional pastoralist gatherings), and policies (a study on policies around the world that enabled pastoralism with positive environmental outcomes). Technical documents have been produced on the economics of pastoralism and on pastoralism as conservation.

Decentralization and land tenure

In many countries decentralisation puts the responsibility for natural resource management in the hands of local people. In Kenya, where farmers have land titles, farmers' investment

---

[1] http://www.iied.org/pubs/search.php?s=MAS.

in their land is a straightforward reflection of their production and consumption decisions. In systems where usufruct rights prevail, this is less the case, although land titles are not necessarily 'better' than the traditional West African systems which are based on intricate patterns of social capital, including trust and kinship. Hilhorst and Baltissen (2004) provide examples of natural resource management at the 'commune' level, such as the planning of trekking routes for pastoralists and their animals that avoid conflict with sedentary farmers.

IIED's Dryland Issue Papers series has a set of studies that describe natural resource management and land tenure at decentralized levels.[2]

1.5 Examples of knowledge management at various levels

KM at local level

Many activities in the field of knowledge management have been implemented at the local level, with local NGOs, producers and extension services. Examples of these are included in this bulletin in Chapters 4 and 5.

KM at national policy level (the Soil Fertility Initiative)

During the mid-1990s, it was felt that each Sub Saharan African (SSA) country would need to identify its own policy, institutional, and above all technical needs, and to develop appropriate responses to address problems of soil fertility and productivity decline. It was against this background that the Soil Fertility Initiative (SFI) for SSA was launched in 1996. SFI's original main objective was to help SSA countries to develop and implement an appropriate, comprehensive, cross-sectoral, and sustained package of activities in response to the declining fertility of their soils; this included the concept of soil fertility 're-capitalization'. There have been various outcomes from this planning effort, including concept papers, pilot projects and fully fledged investment project proposals.

The knowledge needed to formulate national SFI strategies and (national) Country Action Plans generally came from a wide range of national stakeholders who were involved in the process. Often FAO and other SFI partners were involved as well. In Tanzania, insights in learning and knowledge management were integrated into a broader concept of 'Better Land Husbandry'. In some countries, though, there was virtually no follow-up of Action Plans. Implementing soil fertility policies proved to be difficult, as has been documented by Egulu and Ebanyat (2000), who discuss policy processes in Uganda and their impact on soil fertility.[3]

With help from IFDC, the Country Action Plan for Burkina Faso was based on sound knowledge, reflecting investments made during past decades in fertility management and

---

[2] http://www.iied.org/pubs/search.php?s=DIP.
[3] The authors show that research findings are mostly disseminated through publications, seminars and workshops, but they are rarely used by policymakers because most documents are too technical and are only accessible to experts in the subject.

> **Box 5   Coordinating NRM activities**
>
> When the Soil Fertility Initiative's Action Plan for Burkina Faso was drafted, a simultaneous effort was made to draft a national soil management action plan, costing about US$20 million. At the same time, a national action plan for Integrated Water Resources Management had been drafted, also at an estimated cost of US$20 million. But the country is just not in a position to fund both plans at the same time.[1] The water plan was eventually endorsed in 2003, but the soil plan has been put on hold. A joint soil and water action plan might have been more cost-effective, because the overlaps between the two plans are so obvious.
>
> [1] Ministère de l'Agriculture Burkina Faso (1999 ; 2003).

in soil and water conservation. The focus has been on reducing runoff and erosion by using stone rows, grass strips and small dams in gullies, and the practice of *zaï* (planting pits in hardened ironstone surfaces). At the national policy level, however, exchanging knowledge on the various NRM activities proved difficult (see Box 5).

KM on NRM at regional levels in West Africa

KM at a regional West African level is still weak, especially where it depends on collaboration between National Agricultural Research Institutes (NARs). Currently the NARs in the region are in bad shape, due to lack of funding, lack of scientific, development and financial incentives for staff, lack of vision and impact, and lack of KM. There is no tradition of reading books, journals and colleagues' theses, partly as a result of poor internet connectivity and poor access to journals. NGOs and small consultancy enterprises are now mushrooming, taking over responsibilities that used to belong to the NARS. Structural adjustment has dealt a severe blow to the NARS as public institutes contributing to livelihoods. The environment for NARS to survive on their own and grow into agricultural innovation systems is currently anything but enabling.

Regional cooperation would seem essential. Regional approaches may be more cost effective, for example by developing NRM strategies for West African Farming Systems, as depicted in Figure 2.

Information on land and soil at a subcontinent scale

Collecting, processing and displaying information about land and soil quality at a global or continental scale is the mandate of the International Soil Reference and Information Centre (ISRIC). Data are used to support assessments of land degradation and carbon sequestration potential, for example (Batjes, 1995a; 1995b). This is relevant because flexible mechanisms were agreed under the United Nations Framework on Climate Change Convention (UNFCCC). FAO is also a major holder of (sub)continental data.

The World Reference Base for Soil Resources by FAO, ISRIC, and UNESCO, which is at a scale of 1:5 million, is 'the mother' of all soil maps (FAA, 1998). FAO/AGL also has a series of CDs that relate to land management, degradation and rehabilitation. Under the 'SOTER' banner, the FAO and ISRIC jointly put together spatial databases on the

Figure 2   Farming systems in West Africa

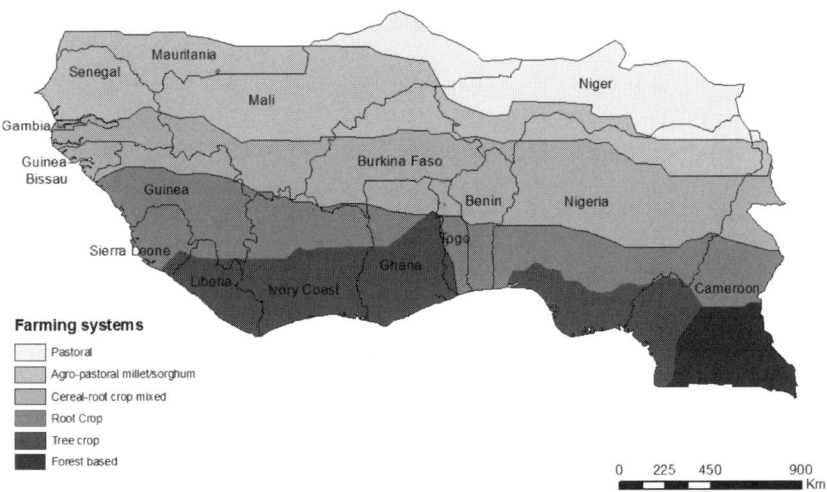

After Dixon and Gulliver (2001) (excluding irrigated, coastal and urban farming systems).

internet.[4] Soil survey data from major UNDP/FAO projects in the 1970s and 1980s are the basis for this database.

1.6   The home-grown approach

Giulio Quaggiotto (2005) of the International Finance Corporation (IFC) argued that the knowledge management approach is now losing ground in the business sector but remains applicable in development. He argues that what accounts for the enduring appeal of knowledge management in development organizations is the stronger motivation for development practitioners – when compared with their counterparts in private companies – to analyse and eventually overcome barriers to knowledge sharing across organizations, communities or even governments in order to maximize their impact on the ground. The fact that development also has its own home-grown approach to knowledge management, illustrated by the work of Paul Engel and others, is indicative that such an approach is fundamentally required in development.

Engel and Salomon (1997) condensed insights in the adoption mechanisms of rural innovations into a Rapid Appraisal of Rural Agricultural Knowledge System (RAAKS) approach. RAAKS has three underlying principles: joint inquiry into the social organization of innovation, multiple analytical perspectives, and social learning. Multi-stakeholder social learning is one of the key issues in later KM activities.

On the basis of more than 25 case studies, they identify configurations in knowledge management for innovation according to their leadership/coordination mechanisms. The main actors and objectives and thus the value of knowledge and of the associated

---

[4]   http://lime.isric.nl/index.cfm?contentid=445.

Figure 3   Social construction of knowledge

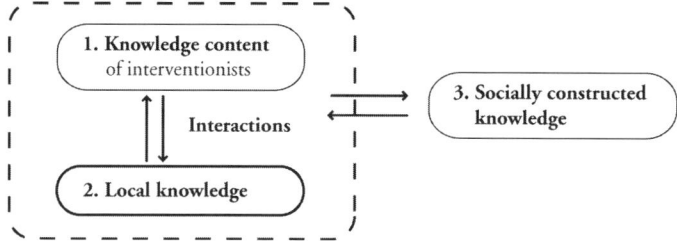

knowledge management differ for these configurations and depend on who is in the driver's seat. They distinguish the following five configurations:
1. Industry-driven KM, which aims to improve efficiency and output quality, and which is generally less sensitive to environmental and social problems.
2. Policy-driven KM, which aims to achieve various policy objectives, is often inflexible and is sometimes used in bureaucratic programmes with many staff, and is often isolated from both knowledge institutes and target groups.
3. Farmer-driven KM, which focuses on farmers' needs, is more or less efficient depending on the quality of the farmer organization, and which is frequently linked to the economic strength of the concerned sector.
4. R&D-driven KM, which aims to advance technical knowledge and improve technical skills, is used at local levels for on-station and on-farm research, but is also used for larger regional studies.
5. Donor-driven KM, which aims to achieve various intervention objectives with external finance and expertise, generally flexible but often lacking institutional sustainability.

Furthermore they analysed a number of case studies on networking for sustainable agriculture driven by NGOs. All have their newsletters, provide services for training and education, and carry out advocacy tasks. In creating space for joint learning and innovation they help to improve inter-organizational knowledge management.

Whoever is the leader, the process of knowledge management in natural resource management often relates to the social construction of knowledge, which is illustrated as in Figure 3.

Thus, knowledge management is not so much regarded as an activity that governs knowledge flows or information management, but is instead as the construction of knowledge through social interactions between different actors.

The four case studies presented in Chapters 2 to 5 will be analysed with this home-grown framework in mind.

2 Knowledge management on soil and water conservation in southern Mali

Floris van der Pol, Ferko Bodnár and Zana Sanogo

Introduction

In 1986, with the support of the Dutch government, a long-term project for soil and water conservation was started in the cotton-growing area of southern Mali. This chapter focuses on the knowledge management aspects of this project, in particular on how the knowledge necessary for the large-scale introduction of soil and water conservation had been developed in the area and how knowledge management was influenced by the changing government and donor policies.

2.1 Introducing soil and water conservation in the cotton-growing area of Mali

This soil and water conservation project (*Projet Lutte Anti Erosive* – PLAE) was created in 1986 within the CMDT (Compagnie Malienne du Développement des Textiles – Malian Textile Development Company), a cotton-development joint-project between the Malian government and a French company. The project's overall objectives were to reduce land degradation, intensify agriculture and improve agricultural production in the cotton-growing area of southern Mali (PLAE, 1986). The main aim was to make the rural population responsible for improving natural resource management (PLAE, 1989; van Mourik et al., 1993; CMDT, 1995). In particular the project aimed to encourage the large-scale adoption of soil and water conservation (SWC) measures that would in the long run allow farmers to become independent from the temporary donor support.

The area

The cotton-growing area in southern Mali (see Figure 4) is about 125,000 km^2, and consists of gentle slopes suitable for cultivation (42%), hill tops with shallow soils not suitable for cultivation, and lower valley land, which is increasingly used for rice cultivation. It contains over 5,000 villages. In 2002 the rural population was estimated at 3.1 million, and was growing by about 2.2% per year. The average population density varies from 20 people per km^2 in the south and west to 37 people per km^2 in the centre and east (extrapolated from CMDT, 1996; MaliArp, 1999). Cotton has long been the main crop in the area. It is grown by around 80% of the farming families, mostly in a two or three-year crop rotation with cereals. About a third of the land area is under cotton. The most common other crops are sorghum, millet, maize, groundnuts, rice and potatoes.

Land degradation

Even though the cultivated fields slope only gently (0-3%), the length of the slopes combined with the poor structure of the loamy-sandy soils and the degraded areas uphill result in water runoff and sheet erosion (Hijkoop et al., 1991), which is estimated to lead to an annual soil loss of 5 to 31 tonnes/ha (Roose, 1985; Hallam and Verbeek, 1986; Bishop and Allen, 1989; Vlot and Traoré, 1994). Moreover, soil nutrient depletion occurs in the region. Van der Pol (1992) calculated nutrient balances under cropping systems in southern Mali and found depletion for nitrogen (at -25 kg N/ha/y) and potassium (at -20 kg K/ha/y). Land degradation was confirmed by comparing vegetation cover in arial photographs from 1952 and 1987 (Jansen and Diarra, 1992). It is not clear if this trend persists, however (see for example Chris Reij in Chapter 3).

Figure 4   The CMDT area (and the OHVN area) in southern Mali

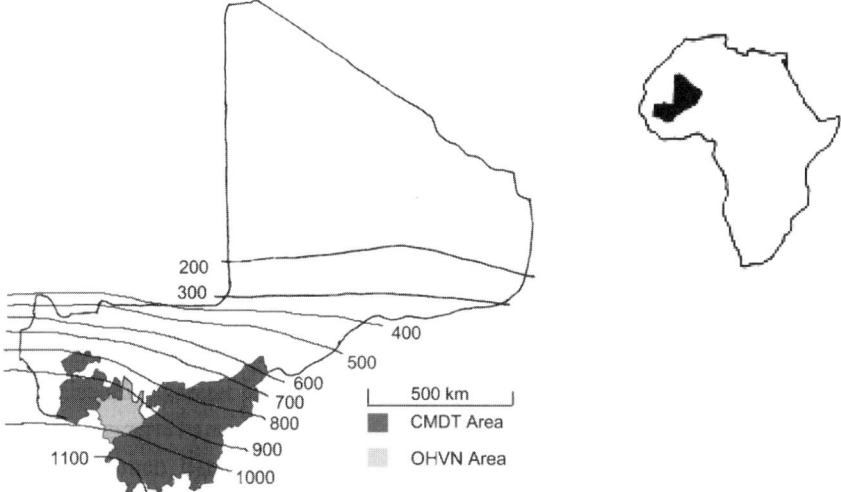

rainfall isohyets in mm, average 1991-2001; CMDT data
(on the right: Mali's location in Africa)

2.2   Knowledge on soil and water conservation in southern Mali, its content and origin

Since 1982, the Malian farming systems research group *(Division de Recherche sur les Systèmes de Production Rurale)* had been testing SWC approaches, including both technical and extension aspects. On the basis of its work with farmers, the group developed technology that was better adapted to real farming conditions than the technology proposed by conventional research. In 1984, following complaints by farmers about decreasing yields and water washing away their crops, trials were carried out in collaboration with the CMDT. The combination of the researchers', CMDT developers' and participating farmers' views finally led to a package of measures that could be adopted by the cotton farmers (Hijkoop et al., 1991; Schrader et al., 1998).

The selected erosion-control measures were a compromise between what was technically desirable and what was compatible with farming practices. An additional consideration was that the approach should not be too complicated for the CMDT extension service to apply. Diversion terraces and protection dikes to block the water would have been difficult to install, demanded specialized personnel and equipment, and were dangerous (because of the risk of the structures collapsing). Therefore semi-permeable erosion-control structures were preferred, such as stone rows installed along the contours above the cultivated area. As different families had fields on the same slope, a village approach was more appropriate than an individual approach. Farmers found it too difficult to cultivate along curved contour lines in their fields and therefore erosion barriers were installed along the field boundaries with the least slopes. These barriers consisted of live fences, grass strips and crop-residue lines. Gullies were reclaimed with stone or crop-residue check dams. Erosion-control measures in the fields included ploughing and sowing across the slope, creating box ridges and dry-season harrowing. The SWC approach took the different units of the toposequence into account (see Figure 5).

Figure 5 Land units in a typical toposequence in Koutiala region and the erosion control measures as applied in Kaniko village

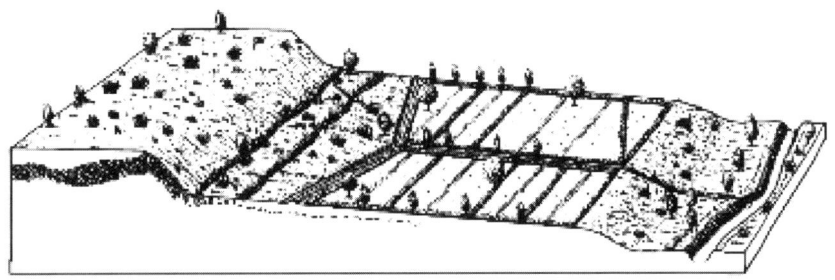

Unit:	Plateau	Escarpment	Glacis	Embankment	Valley
Slope:	0-2%	5-7%	0-2%	0-5%	0-1%
Soil:	Gravel	Stone	Loamy sand	Sandy clay	Clay
Land use:	Pasture, wood	(none)	Annual crops	(none)	Rice, vegetables
SWC:	Regulated use	Protection; Stone rows	Protection dike and drainage canal; Live fences, grass strips, crop residue and stone check dams	Protection	

(Source: Hijkoop et al., 1991).

Additional protective measures were taken above the cultivated glacis. On the escarpment and in some cases on the plateau, the natural vegetation is protected or its exploitation regulated. Collective measures are taken to improve water infiltration or, if necessary, to drain excess water. Individual line and gully interventions are made on the cultivated glacis, mostly on field boundaries. The promotion of erosion control measures was accompanied by the promotion of organic fertilization. A flexible ' basket of options' approach gave farmers a choice of measures and the potential to space out the installation of various measures over several years according to their own capacity (Hallam and van Campen, 1985; Hijkoop et al., 1991).

SWC measures were not the project's only activity. Other components of a broader NRM approach, such as those that addressed soil fertility management, continued to be developed jointly by the project, the CMDT extension service, farmers in participating villages and the farming-systems research group in the area. Recommendations from these research and development activities were tested in pilot extension schemes and where possible translated into training material (Joldersma et al., 1994; Bosma et al., 1996).

2.3   Whose knowledge?

The project was aiming for the large-scale adoption of SWC measures, and used an approach with three specific thrusts: (a) technical: choosing simple, low-cost SWC measures; (b) extension: using a participatory village approach and minimizing farmer dependence on project support and incentives; and (c) institutional: embedding it in phases into the existing extension service to maximize its coverage area (van Campen, 1991; Hijkoop et al., 1991).

The following actors were involved in this approach.

Cotton producers in the region

During the project period about 80% of the rural families in the area grew cotton, with an average farm family cultivating 10 ha of land, or about 0.6 ha per person. Three-quarters of the farm families had at least one plough and two oxen; two-thirds had a donkey cart. On average, each farm family had 10 cattle (including three oxen), four sheep, five goats and 20 chickens. In this region work involving equipment is generally done by men (ploughing, weeding), but during the harvest men, women and children work together in the fields. Farmers generally already knew that erosion partly washed away the fertilizer that they had applied (and sometimes even their crops).

Organization of cotton producers

Since 1977 the CMDT had been encouraging the creation of Village Associations (VA) to which it then transferred administrative tasks regarding credit and cotton payments. Within this context different 'village teams' were organized to carry out various tasks in fields such as health or education, that benefited the whole community. The CMDT paid a percentage of the cotton revenues to the VA, which used the money for community rural development activities and to pay a small fee to the village SWC teams created by the project (Hijkoop, 1991). When the CMDT had to transfer its credit services to official banks that had much less insight into the cotton production of the Villages Associations, many VAs took too much credit, causing the system to collapse.

In 1992, the farmer organization SYCOV *(Syndicat des Producteurs de Coton et Vivriers)* was founded. Presently SYCOV mainly helps to broker fairer negotiations between farmers and the CMDT, thus allowing small farmers to collectively express their views.

The cotton company (CMDT)

The CMDT was for a long time the strongest organization in rural southern Mali and had a dense, multi-layered network of extension workers. About 650 general extension workers covered an average of eight villages each, and 33 district offices helped the general extension workers and formed the link between and with the six regional offices, which were supervised by the National Directorate. The CMDT was owned jointly by the Malian government and the French company CFDT (renamed DAGRIS in 2001), which held respectively 60% and 40% of the shares. It had an integrated dual mission: a commercial mission to produce and process cotton (including provision of inputs and credit, processing, and export) and a public mission to promote rural development (such as agricultural extension, literacy programmes, water supply). This meant that rural development was partly financed by cotton revenues, complemented with support from the Malian government and donor agencies: a 'public-private partnership' before the phrase existed.

Research: Institut d'Economie Rurale (IER)

IER is the main agricultural research institute in Mali and represents more than 70% of the national agricultural research capacity. IER's farming-systems group, started in 1979 at Sikasso (DRSPR: Division de Recherche sur les Systèmes de Production Rurale), was the origin of the soil and water conservation project. At that time it was part of the Ministry of Agriculture, but later on it became an autonomous institute strongly linked with the Ministry of Agriculture.

2.4 Knowledge management activities

The project approach was largely based on sensitization and knowledge management (although this term was not explicitly used when defining the project). Knowledge at farm level was constructed through the dense network of the CMDT extension service (the 650 general extension agents supported by about 45 SWC specialists at various levels), which reached a large number of villages and farmers. The SWC project worked in particular with the village associations promoted by the CMDT, but also with traditional authorities, making use of the strong social coherence in the village, which is typical for southern Mali.

Developing a participatory village approach

The approach, developed in collaboration with a German-funded natural resource management project (Projet Agro Ecology) consisted of a series of chronological steps:
1. Selection of villages and awareness raising using a participatory rural appraisal module. During the first awareness meeting in the village, villagers discussed past, present and future land use. Then the villagers were asked how motivated they were to take on an SWC programme. The SWC specialist selected villages based on the actual erosion risk and on the motivation of the villagers.
2. Constitution and training of a SWC village team (five active farmers, at least two of whom were literate were trained during five days), field visits and slide shows.

3. Erosion diagnosis and planning of erosion control, collective installation of erosion control measures, and evaluation.
4. Supplementary five-day training in soil fertility management for interested farmers in the targeted villages (this step was added later, in 1995).
5. Use of mass media (radio) to reach farmers in all villages. In a later stage, more emphasis was given to the training of SWC village teams, the erosion diagnosis and the planning of SWC activities.

By the end of the development of the approach, in 1989, farmers in 36 villages in two of the five CMDT regions had been trained and had undertaken SWC activities.

Scaling up

The approach described above was used in two subsequent project phases:

(a) Capacity building
From 1989-1996, the SWC project invested heavily in building the capacity of the CMDT staff. The CMDT recruited additional personnel who followed the project's SWC training and were then placed in the CMDT multidisciplinary teams, initially at the district level, later also at the regional level. Each new district SWC specialist was paired with a general extension worker. They started working in one village, gradually increasing the number of villages and eventually involving all general extension workers. The approach was at high cost at the beginning, but ensured long-run impact. In 1992, the SWC project became a CMDT division, retaining project financial support (Schrader, 1997). In 1996, all extension staff were trained in both SWC and soil fertility management. The number of villages in which farmers had been trained and that had undertaken SWC activities increased from 36 in 1990 to 1,135 in 1996 (Schrader and Wennink, 1996).

(b) Handing over (1996-2002)
In 1996 the Dutch donor switched from a project approach to a programme approach. As a result the SWC project became a component in the rural development programme, for which the CMDT received financial support. Whereas up to 1994 SWC activities had been concentrated in the targeted SWC villages, from 1996 onwards SWC extension became more diluted, and was promoted by the general extension workers. The number of villages trained in SWC increased from 1,135 in 1996 to 2,562 in 2000, representing 51% of the 5,054 villages in southern Mali (Bodnár and de Graaff, 2003). In addition, general extension workers gave SWC advice on a more ad hoc or even individual basis, including in villages that did not receive the full SWC extension package. As a result, in 2002 erosion control measures were laid out in 94% of the villages, on 46% of the farms and in 15% of the fields (CMDT, 2003). In total 23,000 km of hedgerows had been planted and 7,500 km of stone rows had been installed by 2000 (Bodnár et al., 2006).

The Dutch government stopped financial support in 1998 and technical assistance at the end of 1999. The German NRM programme ended at the beginning of 2002. From 2000 onwards, the CMDT faced a financial crisis and gradually had to decrease its budget for the SWC extension programme, leaving the SWC teams without proper financial resources.

Evaluation by producers

In 2003, farmers in five targeted villages ranked the activities in which they had participated in order of importance (Bodnár et al., 2006). These included a limited number of complementary incentives that had been given by the project.[5] The activity the farmers ranked as most important was the creation of awareness about erosion, followed by training of an SWC village team, diagnosis of erosion problems, planning of erosion control and training in soil fertility management. The incentives were the least appreciated. Apparently, farmers valued highly the knowledge services provided by the project. According to them, the SWC village team played an important role in the first years after they had been trained, but often stopped functioning later.

2.5 Strategic knowledge management aspects

Initial organisation of knowledge management

The SWC project's initial approach was to integrate as much as possible the project activities and associated knowledge flows into the CMDT structure (see Figure 6). This fitted well with the mission of the CMDT, which was in that period a private-public organization with a strong mandate in extension and natural resource management. The integration of the project into the CMDT improved over time (see dotted box in Figure 6).

Within the context described the organisation of knowledge management worked fairly well, as can be concluded from the high adoption of SWC measures in the area.

There were problems with the decreasing functionality of the village SWC teams. This happened because village authority weakened, members of the SWC village team were not paid, and the working groups failed to show up for collective work. Proposed solutions were: paying the SWC village team, renewing the SWC village team, or installing several SWC village teams in larger villages where collective action was problematic. In 1998, the CMDT proposed that the Village Associations pay SWC village team members from their cotton revenue, but most did not. During that period, many VAs had debt problems and split up into several smaller VAs. This decreased the social cohesion at the village level and complicated the work of the SWC village team. Although some farmers preferred individual training, most thought that training an SWC village team was more effective and more efficient. But even with the proposed adaptations, until

---

[5] Initially each trained SWC village team received a water-tube level to peg contour markers. After 2000, line levels were sold to individual farmers. Where insufficient planting material was available, the SWC programme supplied Euphorbia balsamifera cuttings and Jatropha curcas seed for live fences and Andropogon gayanus seed for grass strips. Initially, the seed was free; later, it was sold to farmers. During the pilot and promotion phases an annual SWC contest was organized to financially and socially reward the most active villages. In 1995 this contest had become too strong an incentive and was replaced by 'environment days', with field visits but without prizes. Under the SWC programme special credit was available for donkey carts that facilitated the production and transport of compost and wire netting for building improved cattle pens. Although farmers paid back the credit, the revolving funds stopped functioning in 2000 due to poor financial administration by CMDT.

Figure 6   Knowledge flows according to the initial project strategy

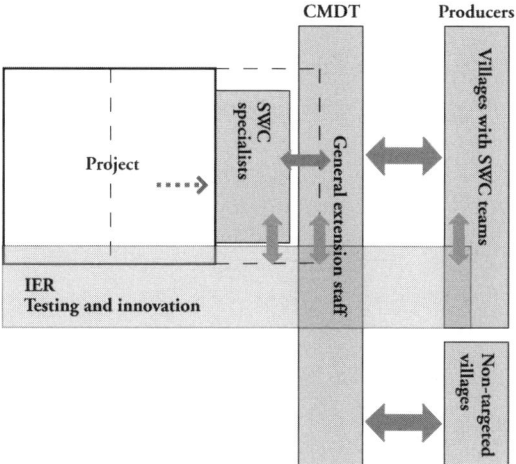

arrows = knowledge exchange generated through the project;
dotted box = integration of the project into the CMDT
improved over time.

1999 the project strategy remained completely based on the role of CMDT in the rural communities.

A changing context

In the mean time, especially following World Bank interventions that aimed to liberalize rural services, the strong role of CMDT in the organization of cotton production – and in particular in erosion control and in securing sustainability of cotton production – was reversed. The commercial activities related to cotton were consigned to several privatised companies, leaving the rural development activities to the other actors: the national and local governments, farmer organizations and private organizations. This finally led to the dismissal of the SWC specialists and of a large number of general extension workers at the CMDT. Furthermore the government's decentralisation policy shifted responsibility for NRM to the rural communities, who created NRM committees that focused mainly on the uses of forests and other common resources. Their priorities did not always matching those of the CMDT village SWC teams. Not much emphasis was put on SWC measures in the farmers' fields.

The project's KM approach did not anticipate these developments. Although it became clear that other players, like NGOs and local authorities, would have to take over CMDT's rural development tasks, including SWC, no KM strategy was prepared to enable the continuation of the approach in the new context. Five factors hampered the preparation of such a strategy:
• The project donor support was channelled uniquely to the CMDT. The CMDT in turn contracted the technical assistance.
• In the new, fragmented, multi-actor context there was no leading partner who could organize SWC activities and feel responsibility for such a programme.

- The major donors in the SWC sector withdrew their support.
- The main knowledge institute (IER) that had developed the SWC technologies was strongly linked to the Ministry of Agriculture, while the government attributed responsibility for soil and water conservation to the Ministry of Environment.
- The Dutch government withdrew its general support to the agricultural sector and refocused it partly on the Ministry of Environment with a programme that focused more on maintaining community areas (biodiversity, pastures, fire prevention) than on soil and water conservation in farmer's fields.

In 2004, a number of private consultants and NGOs were active in the field of SWC. Some organizations had been founded by former CMDT SWC specialists and general extension workers, but many new actors also started up, without much knowledge on the technical and managerial aspects of SWC. Some of the NGOs asked the Dutch government to help them with Dutch technical assistance. In this new context, the local capacity that had been built was not used well.

Knowledge management in the new context

In 2005, part of the remaining budget of the Dutch support to agricultural research was used to mitigate this sub-optimal use of knowledge on and experience of soil and water conservation. The 'Centre for Information and Knowledge Management on the Environment' (CGICE) was created at IER's Research Centre in southern Mali (Sikasso). The Centre was to operate in a multi-actor environment (see Figure 7).

Figure 7   How the Centre for Information and Knowledge Management on the Environment works

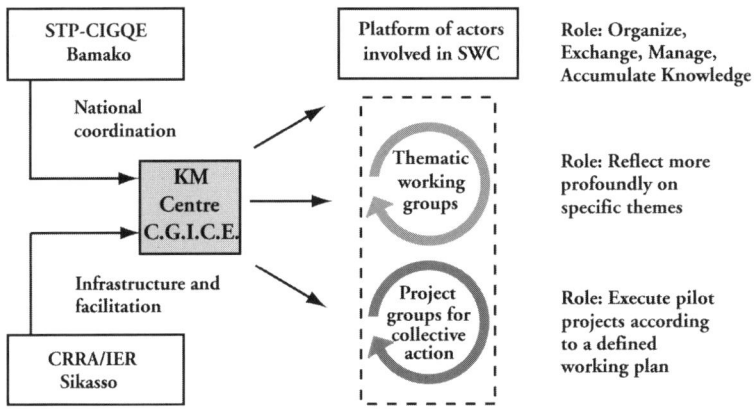

The Permanent Technical Secretariat of the Institutional Framework for the Management of Environmental Questions (STP/CIGQE) of the Ministry of Environment would be responsible for national coordination, ensuring that the CGICE would operate in accordance with the National Policy for Environmental Protection and related activities. The other partners were the producer organizations and their confederations (such as SYCOV), Economic Interest Groups, the Chamber of Agriculture, NGOs, private enterprises (CMDT, transporters, input providers, import/export service providers), and local government structures.

During a start-up workshop with a number of these actors, the following activities were proposed:
1. Create platforms and networks that support the exchange of information between the various actors intervening in the fields of soil fertility and SWC.
2. Capture and publish all important CMDT information on soil fertility management and SWC on a CD.
3. Update knowledge on soil fertility management and SWC through data collection, studies and research.
4. Update and develop training modules for extension services, NGOs and producers, and organize related training.
5. Evaluate appropriation by producers of popularized soil fertility management and SWC technologies.

In October 2005, a general workshop was organized to allow the various actors involved in soil fertility management and SWC to define and confirm their main KM constraints. Knowledge constraints were identified in the areas of soil fertility management (reasons for declining cotton yields), soil and water conservation (SWC measures barely included in the 'Communities Socio-Economic Development Plans' nor in the 'Communities Environmental Action Plans'; if included often poorly executed; declining adoption) and conflict management (laws concerning NRM were not well-known by actors involved in NRM).

Due to insufficient support of the Centre by the Ministry of Environment and a lack of interest by producer organizations and donors, its activities stopped in 2007.

Issues for knowledge management strategies

Three important questions need to get attention in developing good strategic knowledge management. These are discussed in the following paragraphs.

- Who could organize knowledge management?

Knowledge management appears to be strongly influenced by the policy environment. Within a large company with a public mandate and engaged in commercial smallholder agriculture, they way CMDT was when the SWC project began, it was possible to achieve results by implementing an approach based on awareness raising and knowledge management. In the current liberalized but fragmented multi-stakeholder environment knowledge management is much more difficult. Even the knowledge base built up during the SWC project seems to have degraded. Much is expected from producer organizations, but their knowledge management capacity is still weak. There is also renewed interest in establishing public-private partnerships that could take care of knowledge management.

- Sharing knowledge?

KM involves different actors. Government actors at all levels of the decentralised structures, producers and their organisations, knowledge institutes, NGOs, private-sector enterprises and donors: all have a part of the knowledge that they share. The question is whether individual actors are prepared to share knowledge so that the total knowledge base could be exploited. This is not yet a tradition for these actors, but its need is increasingly being recognized at higher policy levels.

- KM only?

Even though the project had many positive results, it is questionable whether the strong project focus on awareness raising and KM did not hamper the development of sound institutional and financial mechanisms. The project barely addressed important areas such as taxes and subvention and laws and regulations for the use of land. As a result there are no rules to protect farmed land, SWC measures are not really included in the Communities Socio-Economic Development Plans nor in the Communities Environmental Action Plans, and there is no mechanism in place to translate the long-term economic and social benefits of better land use into financial incentives for soil conservation measures. Without being cemented into this policymaking context it is unsure whether the adoption of SWC measures can be sustained. While an awareness raising and KM approach can be efficient in mobilizing large numbers of people, to get sustainable results it needs to be combined with sound institutional and financial measures.

2.6 Conclusions

With substantial project support to the public activities of a private enterprise (CMDT), soil and water conservation measures have been introduced on a large scale in the cotton-growing area of southern Mali. This was achieved particularly by massively increasing knowledge about how to combat soil erosion and maintain productivity. The increased knowledge was highly appreciated by the producers in the area, more so than other incentives given away by the project to promote soil and water conservation.

It is still not clear what is the best way to promote knowledge management (sharing and accumulation of experiences) in a liberalized multi-stakeholder environment, and remains a major challenge. This case study gives no reason for optimism in this respect. Another challenge is to find the right mix of knowledge management activities and financial and institutional mechanisms that is necessary to sustain results.

Sharing knowledge between all actors involved in soil and water conservation, that is national and local governments, donors, NGOs, producers and their organizations needs to be organized more systematically in order to sustain the productive capacity of the farmers' land in the long run.

3 Farmer-managed natural regeneration in Niger: a case study in knowledge management

Chris Reij, Mahamane Larwanou, Adam Toudou and Yamba Boubabcar

Introduction

In August 2005 the Center for International Cooperation of VU University of Amsterdam (CIS) and the *Centre Régional pour l'Enseigment Supérieur en Agriculture* (CRESA) of the Faculty of Agronomy of the University of Niamey launched a multidisciplinary study to identify long-term trends in agriculture and environment in Niger and to analyse the economic impacts of different natural resource management techniques used in Niger. This study was implemented by a substantial team of about 10 national researchers, who were supported by a remote-sensing specialist from the United States Geological Survey (USGS) Data Center for EROS (South Dakota). The study was funded by the Swiss Agency for Development and Cooperation (SDC) and by the United States Agency for Aid and Development (USAID). The latter funded contributions by the USGS Data Center for EROS, but also by the Washington-based International Resources Group (IRG). CILSS, the Inter-State Agency for Drought Control in the Sahel, actively supported the study.

The study generated some interesting and sometimes unexpected results. It made clear that the Government of Niger and its funding partners had invested substantially in the rehabilitation of degraded land using a range of both simple and more complex water-harvesting techniques, including *zaï*, half moons, contour stone bunds, earth bunds, and trenches. The most spectacular finding of this study was that since the mid-1980s farmers, in particular in regions with high population densities like Maradi and three departments of the Zinder region (Magaria, Matameye and Mirriah), have systematically protected natural regeneration on their farmland. The scale at which they have done this increased during the study as more remote sensing images became available and more field visits were made. In September 2006 it was assumed that the area covered by this farmer-managed natural regeneration was at least 3 million ha. Now, after additional remote-sensing work (analysis of aerial photos and high-resolution satellite images) and field visits, Gray Tappan of USGS, South Dakota (Tappan, 2009) estimates that the on-farm re-greening covers at least 5 million ha.

The spectacular scale of farmer-managed natural regeneration in Niger seems to have been largely overlooked until 2006. There are one or two articles about this phenomenon in the Maradi region, but not a single publication could be found about this re-greening in parts of the Zinder region, which covers at least 1 million ha and is strongly dominated by *Faidherbia albida*, a nitrogen-fixing species.

A communication strategy was developed from the beginning of the study. Everyone involved felt that the results should be presented to a wider public in Niger, Europe and the USA, but also to policymakers in both government and donor agencies.

3.1 Re-greening the Sahel

The process

A comparison of aerial photos from 1975 and satellite images from 2002-03 or more recent photos of the selected study villages in 2006 revealed that most villages have many more trees now than 30 years ago. This went against the widely shared perception that the number of trees had declined strongly from their having been cut for firewood or to enable the expansion of farmland. Several study villages have 15 to 20 times more trees in 2003 than in 1975 despite a large increase in population. Photo 1 shows the village of Galma (in the southern part of the Maggia valley, Tahoua region) in 1975 and in 2003. The black dots are mature trees. It is obvious that there were many more trees in 2003 than in 1975.

Photo 1   The village of Galma in 1975 and in 2003 (more people, more trees)

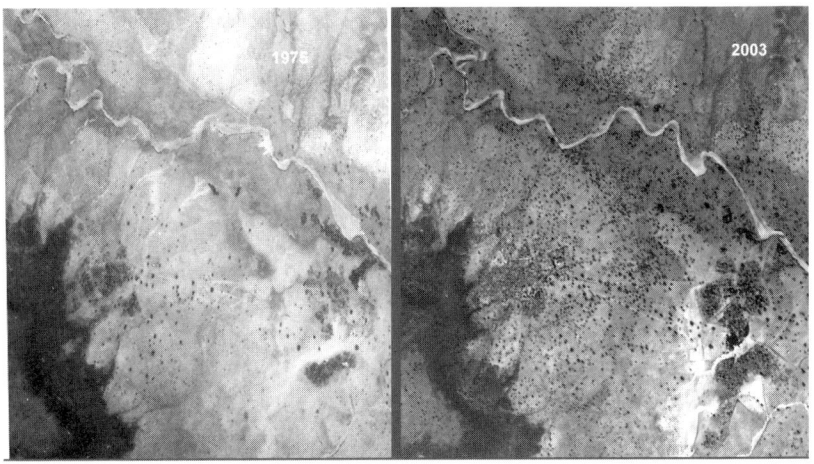

Photo courtesy of Gray Tappan, USGS Data Center for EROS, South Dakota.

The trees are scattered randomly on the fields, which indicates that they have not been planted, but that trees regenerating spontaneously in the farmers' fields have been selected according to the farmer's preferences and protected against livestock grazing and cutting. The young trees are also pruned to allow them to develop a main trunk. In this way farmers determine how many trees they want to grow on their fields and where.

Which species regenerate depends on farmer preferences, on specific site conditions (rainfall, soils), on the existing underground root systems, and on the seed stock. The most common ones include: *Faidherbia albida* (nitrogen-fixing, fodder), *Combretum spp.* (firewood), *Piliostigma reticulatum* (fodder, soil fertility improvement), *Adansonia digitata* (baobab), *Acacia Senegal* (Arabic gum), and *Balanites aegyptiaca*. In the densely populated parts of the Zinder region, *Faidherbia albida* is almost a monoculture, but in parts of the Maradi region the diversity of trees is increasing, in part because farmers have begun re-introducing species which had disappeared during the droughts of the 1970s and 1980s.

The protection and management of trees is more a social than a technical process and can only succeed if farmers manage to control grazing on their fields for some years, which means that they have to invest labour in supervising the livestock and the fields. They will only do so when this generates tangible benefits. Farmers in the Zinder and Maradi regions have identified a wide range of positive socio-economic, biophysical and climate impacts from re-greening based on their protection and management of trees.

The regeneration of communal areas is more complex. In the Aguié department (Maradi region) an IFAD-funded project created 'Village Committees for the Management of Regeneration and Sylvo-Pastoral Areas'. One problem is that villages that have invested in natural regeneration have to protect it against intrusions from outsiders from villages who have not made the same investment (most likely due to social conflicts), and against the uncontrolled lopping of branches by herders transiting these areas. Such village committees do not seem to exist in the densely populated parts of the Zinder region, however, possibly because farmer-managed natural regeneration is so common.

A short exploratory study was undertaken in the Zinder region in June 2006 (Larwanou et al., 2006) to identify what had triggered the farmers to begin protecting and managing the young trees on their fields. Most farmers interviewed mentioned that they had to fight the "Sahara", by which they did not mean sand dunes rolling southwards, but the strong dust and sand storms. The environmental and economic crisises of the 1970s and 1980s appears to have catalysed the farmers into action. In some regions NGO projects seem to have played a key role in catalysing farmer-managed natural regeneration. This has been the case in the Maradi region, for example, where during the drought years of 1984 and 1985 an NGO (Sudan Interior Mission) offered food-for-work to farmers protecting young trees, but elsewhere (in the Zinder region, for example), the process seems to have been more spontaneous, but may well have some cultural roots, as *Faidherbia albida* had been vigorously protected by the sultans in the early twentieth century. A major difference between 1985 and 2006 is also that the perception in 1985 was that all trees belonged to the state; whereas in 2006 most farmers felt that they had exclusive rights to the trees on their fields.

Socio-economic impacts

Re-greening with woody species produces a wide range of socio-economic impacts. This includes an impact on **poverty reduction**: with more trees on farm fields, total plant production increases (higher crop yields, increased fodder production), which makes it possible to keep more livestock, sell more firewood, etc. and thus leads to higher incomes for poor rural households. A 10% increase in total agricultural production in Africa is reported to reduce rural poverty between 6% and 9% (Irz, et al. 2002).

Re-greening is about capital creation, which can be illustrated by using the example of Niger again. The number of trees per hectare varies, but an average of 40 small and larger trees/ha is a reasonable estimate. Using the estimate from the introduction to this chapter of 5 million hectare 're-greened', this means that on-farm re-greening covers 200 million trees. If the average annual value produced by a tree in terms of fodder, firewood, fruit, medicinal products, soil fertility, etc. is about 1 Euro/tree/year (which is probably an underestimate, see data of World Resources Institute 2008, p. 150), then the annual value produced by the new trees is in the order of 200 million Euros/year, which basically goes straight into the farmers' pockets. This estimate does not yet include the value of the standing tree stock.

Another important impact of re-greening is its contribution to **reducing vulnerability to drought**. In 2005 villages in Niger that had invested in tree protection and management were better able to cope with the consequences of the 2004 drought and had lower infant mortality rates than villages that had not done so. Villagers were able to cut some trees and sell them as firewood, which generated some cash allowing farmers to buy expensive cereals. They were also able to harvest more edible fruits and leaves. Because the trees produced fodder they also had more livestock and lower livestock mortality rates. The 2005 famine meant a lot of hardship, including for villages with trees, but not surprisingly they were better able to cope with the effects of the drought than villages with fewer trees.

Re-greening increases the production of fruits, nuts, and edible leaves and in this way it also leads to **improved nutrition**, which means better health. Better developed tree-based production systems produce a more varied diet, a return to more traditional foods including forest products. It also means an increased ability to rely on edible tree products when the annual crops fail. Drought, insect attack, weeds, etc., which can severely reduce annual crop yields usually have much lower negative impacts on perennial tree species. The leaves of certain species, for instance of *Maeru crassifolia*, contain a lot of vitamin A. The impact of farmer-managed natural regeneration on nutrition requires more research.

In some regions in Niger and Burkina Faso natural forests have virtually disappeared and women can no longer rely on natural forests for firewood. They now depend almost entirely on the trees they grow on the land cultivated by their family. It is striking that in the densely populated parts of Zinder women now spend on average only half an hour each day collecting firewood and all firewood is produced on the cultivated fields. Twenty years ago firewood collection required on average 2.5 hours/day (Larwanou et al., 2006). **It is obvious that more on-farm trees mean a considerable reduction in the work burden of women and children.**

Finally, and also of vital importance, is that agroforestry does seem to lead to a **reduction in the number of conflicts between herders and farmers**. Although the sample of villages studied was small, a study in Niger shows a substantial reduction in conflicts (by about 80%) between herders and farmers in villages that had invested in improved natural resource management (Baoua, 2006). This is not surprising, because the natural resource "cake" has increased, not contracted. More fodder means that there is more to share. It does not mean that conflicts have disappeared and in drought years they are likely to increase again. Farmers in Zinder said that when herders cut branches for their livestock the leaves are used as fodder, but the some of the wood is left on the ground, which is subsequently collected by the women.

Biophysical impacts

Experience in Niger shows increased integration by farmers of trees, crops and livestock, which leads to more complex and productive farming systems. More fodder means more livestock, and because livestock is managed more intensively, it also leads to more manure and **improved soil fertility management**. Twenty years ago farmers in the Magaria and Matameye departments (Zinder region) used manure as a source of household energy, but now all the manure is used to fertilize the fields (Larwanou et al., 2006). The current practice of farmer management of natural resources also leads to **increased biodiversity**. For instance, the village of Dan Saga in Niger's Maradi region, which had few trees and few species left in the 1980s, now has 35 different woody species and villagers are re-introducing indigenous species that had disappeared in the 1970s and 80s (Larwanou and Saadou, 2006).

Climate impacts

According to farmers in Niger's Maradi and Zinder regions, they **suffer less from dust storms** than they did 20 years ago, and early in the rainy season the current high tree densities protect their crops better against the impact of strong winds. Before, it was not uncommon for farmers to have to re-sow their annual crops four to six times because of sand blasting and burial during wind storms. Farmers now clearly perceive an improved micro-climate. During the 2007 rainy season the rains in Niger arrived late and stopped early. Yet the indication is that farmers in the Maradi and Zinder regions with many trees on their fields have a better harvest than those who have not. The simple reason is that they just needed to sow once, which increased the length of the growing season. What is happening in Niger is a great example of better coping with drought and drier conditions. There is much talk about adapting to climate change, but farmers in the Sahel have been adapting not only by maintaining trees in their fields, but also through the systematic use of quick-maturing crop varieties or through the introduction of simple water-harvesting techniques that increase yields and yield security.

Data will soon be available for what the re-greening of parts of Niger means in terms of quantities of carbon sequestered.[6] The first indications are that it is significant, and that there are measurable increases in soil carbon under the increased tree cover in farmer's fields.

3.2   Where knowledge goes

The current state of knowledge regarding farmer-managed natural regeneration

Scientific knowledge on farmer-managed natural regeneration in Niger is still superficial, which is not surprising as the scale of this phenomenon has just recently been uncovered.

---

[6]   A report is in preparation by Tappan, Larwanou and Guero.

As described in the previous section, farmers have attributed a wide range of impacts to the re-greening, but these have not yet been adequately quantified.[7] It can be argued that farmers have been gaining new knowledge about trees and their management since the environmental crises of the 1970s and 1980s. Some knowledge they have developed themselves through experiential learning, and new knowledge has also been introduced by projects. Before the 1970s rainfall levels were higher and population densities lower. In the regions with the highest population densities useful on-farm trees were systematically protected, but in regions with low population densities the bush and land under long fallow produced sufficient firewood, fodder, fruits and nuts. The droughts and high rates of population growth sparked a process of agricultural intensification (Mortimore et al., 2000).

Whose knowledge?

Is the knowledge about trees and their management spread equally among the young, the old, men and women? Are all different ethnic groups protecting and managing trees or is it is a specific group? These questions are difficult to answer, but some general observations can be made. Women have an intimate knowledge of trees as they use them for several purposes. Many farm households are female-headed as men have migrated to work. This means in many cases that decisions about farm management are taken by women. Men and women can also own and buy and sell trees, although the scale at which this is happening is unknown.

Knowledge about tree management does not seem to be limited to specific ethnic groups. During the survey in the Zinder region one of the most striking examples of farmer-managed natural regeneration was found in a *Bouzou* village. The *Bouzou* are *haussa*-speaking Tuareg who settled decades ago in this region. They own a lot of livestock, which means that they can adequately fertilize their fields and they rarely have to cut trees during a drought year to generate cash for buying cereals.

The *Haussa* in Northern Nigeria do not seem to protect and manage trees on their fields, whereas the *Haussa* north of the border in Niger do so systematically. One reason for this might be that Northern Nigeria is richer and people rely less on agriculture than they do in Niger. In any case, the difference in tree densities north and south of the Niger-Nigeria border is striking and can easily be seen on satellite images. Additional research is required to really understand the causes of this difference.

Knowledge flows: communicating the findings of the study

Knowledge concerning the findings of the study flows in several directions:
- from the study team to national and international levels;
- from the study team to farmers and vice versa;
- from international and national levels to farmers and vice versa; and
- from farmer to farmer.

---

[7] A research team of the University of Niamey is now trying to quantify some of the impacts.

In the next sections we try to analyse the various flows.

From the study team to national and international levels
As soon as preliminary data from the Niger study became available they were used to spread the message that contrary to the usual doom and gloom stories about the Sahel in general and Niger in particular, some positive environmental trends had been identified.

Several activities were already underway on the basis of the preliminary findings before the formal presentation of the findings at a workshop for national policymakers in Niamey in September 2006. These included:

- An editor from the BBC Environment Series was approached in November 2005 with the following story...

    "The BBC showed pictures in August 2005 of women and starving children in feeding centers, but there's a very different story to tell about farmers in Niger who have been successfully fighting land degradation."

This led to a positive reaction and in March 2006 a Swiss film team went to Niger to make a documentary about desertification and land rehabilitation in Niger, which was shown on BBC World in December 2006 as part of the series "Villages on the Frontline". According to the editor this programme was also broadcast by other TV channels around the world and watched by about 240 million people.

- In February 2006 the preliminary findings were presented at an international seminar in Geneva organized by Swiss Development Cooperation on Drought, Hunger and Desertification.

In terms of communicating the final results, September and October 2006 were the key months:
- All members of the national study team presented their findings in a two-day workshop in Niamey, which was attended by about 60 people, including technical staff from ministries, and representatives of donor agencies, NGOs and farmer organizations. The Executive Secretary of CILSS and several of his staff participated for the full two days. As only a few participants were aware of the findings before the workshop, most participants were surprised.
- Two days later an international seminar took place in Niamey, organized by ICRISAT and ICARDA, on a new research initiative called from "Desert to Oasis". The organizers had invited Mahamane Larwanou and Chris Reij to jointly open the presentations with the findings of the Niger study. Many presenters subsequently referred to the Niger study. The seminar organizers created opportunities to spread the message further, including an interview with a *New Scientist* journalist and the presentation of the findings of the study to the Prime Minister of Niger.
- A short article was published in *New Scientist* in October 2006, which led to a small stream of articles in European newspapers, including one in a Swiss tabloid. The press exposure after the New Scientist article resulted in further communication of the results of the study internationally.

- It drew the attention of Paul Salopek, a *Chicago Tribune* journalist (and Pulitzer Prize Winner), who in the process of preparing an article about the Sahel for *National Geographic* met with members of the research team in Niamey and visited Zinder.
- Early in January 2007 Salopek told Lydia Polgreen, the bureau chief of the *New York Times* in West Africa, about the environmental transformation in Niger. She was briefed in Dakar before leaving for a 10-day visit to Niger. While in Niger she was accompanied by Mahamane Larwanou, the study team's forester-ecologist. This resulted in a front page article in the *New York Times* on 11 February, 2007 (the Sunday edition, which sells 1.7 million copies).
- This article was also printed in the *International Herald Tribune* on the same day and the next weekend in the English insert in *Le Monde*. The article was quoted in a range of newspapers around the world (for instance in *The Age* in Australia). After that National Public Radio in the US sent a reporter to Niger who visited sites accompanied by Gray Tappan, the study's remote-sensing specialist, and Larwanou. A 30-minute programme was broadcast in July 2007 (about 30 million listeners).

At the national level, results have been communicated in various ways.
- Niger's national television station, private television channels, and the national and private radio stations have all reported the study and interviewed members of the national study team.
- The offices of the Prime Minister and the President requested copies of the report. In January, President Tandja mentioned the results of the study extensively in his annual address to the diplomatic corps. The Prime Minister mentioned the findings in his statements and the Minister of Environment used the information in a speech on national television. The President has a printed copy of the Power Point presentation of the study, which he is said to show to all development-relevant visitors.

At the regional level:
- CILSS, which was involved in the study from the start and is coordinating a similar study in three other Sahelian countries, presented the findings in meetings of all ministers of agriculture and environment of the CILSS member countries.

At the scientific level the study findings have been presented by the team at different international conferences, including:
- in the plenary as well as at a side-event of the UNCCD CRIC meeting in Buenos Aires (March 2007);
- the economic aspects were presented at an international seminar on the costs of land degradation held at IFAD, Rome (December 2006); and
- in an international UNDP-DDC organized seminar in Nairobi as well as in a CGIAR workshop with representatives of the other CGIAR centres, including IFPRI, ICARDA, ICRISAT, ICRAF, and CIMMYT.

From the study team to farmers and vice versa
During the study the villagers were the teachers and the researchers the students who engaged in a dialogue with the farmers about the reported trends and impacts. Members of the study team have subsequently re-visited several study villages accompanied by journalists and other visitors, which is perceived by the villagers as a sign of national and

international recognition. This has instilled a sense of pride in what they have managed to achieve. The villages that were covered by new low-altitude aerial photos received a copy.

The results of the study have not been systematically reported back to all the participating villages. This is expensive and was not budgeted for.

From the national and international level to farmers and vice versa
The farmers of several (study and non-study) villages have received a number of national and international visitors, including journalists, researchers, donor agency staff and NGO staff. One striking example was when the director of a Mexican NGO working on reforestation travelled to Niger to learn from the farmer-managed natural regeneration experience.

From farmer to farmer

No farmer-to-farmer exchange visits took place as part of the study. However, inspired by the study findings, a new initiative has now been developed that will use farmer-to-farmer visits as a key activity. The visits will be between farmers in Niger, but also between farmers in other countries in the Sahel (see Section 3.3).

3.3 The impact of knowledge on farmer-managed natural regeneration

Using the results for teaching and training

At a national level, the members of the Niger study team are using all opportunities to plough back into research and training the results of the study. They do so systematically in the regular teaching programmes of the University of Niamey, which include courses in agroforestry, soil science, agronomy, human geography and biogeography and student field work. In this way hundreds of students have already been exposed to the results of the study. At a regional level the results are used in the training courses held at AGHRYMET in Niamey on the role of agroforestry in Sahelian production systems and on NRM and food security in the Sahel.

Thus participants from nine countries in the Sahel were informed about the findings.

Using the results to inspire other studies

Although the Niger study identified the process of re-greening in some regions of Niger and identified a wide range of impacts, it did not go far enough in quantifying the impacts of farmer-managed natural regeneration on rural poverty reduction and on household food security (MDG 1) or on gender. For this reason a short new study was launched in August 2007, funded by IIED and involving 12 students from the University of Niamey whose fieldwork is supervised by six former study team members.
In 2007 similar CILSS-coordinated studies in Burkina Faso, Mali and Senegal were launched. These new country studies drew some precious lessons from the experience of the Niger study.

From research to action

The large-scale re-greening in Niger, which is mainly the result of farmers protecting and managing natural regeneration, has inspired the formulation of a new regional initiative for the re-greening of the Sahel. The members of an international alliance of NGOs and research organizations will jointly promote farmer-managed natural regeneration in the Sahel by building on existing grassroots success stories in on-farm re-greening. A first meeting of this new international alliance took place in London in September 2007 and since then the first steps have been taken to build national alliances of stakeholders (NGOs and other partners) in Senegal, Mali, Burkina Faso and Niger (Reij, 2008). It is felt that the time is ripe for a substantive initiative in this field in the Sahel given the multiple impacts on poverty reduction, adaptation to climate change, biodiversity and household food security. Moving from research to action to improve the livelihoods of the rural poor in the Sahel is the logical and desired outcome of the Niger study.

3.4   Conclusions

From the beginning the intention was not to produce a report that would simply decorate bookshelves, but to communicate the results to national and international policymakers and to the widest possible public in and outside the Sahel. This was done without an explicit knowledge management strategy, sometimes creating opportunities and other times grasping opportunities that presented themselves. It has all been achieved despite limited financial resources. Its success was mainly due to a combination of good fortune and the readiness of researchers to invest considerable time in informing both policymakers and journalists and in accompanying them to the field. Much time and energy has also been invested in presenting the results in international fora. This effort may have resulted in a slow change in perception about current trends in the Sahel at the level of researchers as well as national and international policymakers. More people are now aware that success stories can be found in the Sahel than before this study.

The Niger study identified some trends in agriculture and environment, but it was a fairly small and short-term study[8] that generated some new knowledge and insights but also triggered a number of additional policy research needs. One of the key challenges is to adequately quantify the multiple impacts of farmer-managed natural regeneration, and a start was made to do so a year after the study ended.

The study inspired the formulation of a new civil society initiative for the re-greening of the Sahel, which will build on grassroots success stories in farmer-managed natural regeneration in Niger and elsewhere in the Sahel. Even if the study has not had an immediate impact on current projects and policies in Niger, its results will lead to substantive action on the ground.

---

[8] The study lasted one year and cost about 275,000, including the costs of national and international researchers, fieldwork and a national workshop for policymakers.

4 Knowledge management in an integrated soil fertility management project in Togo

Constant Dangbégnon[9], Suzanne Nederlof, Adonko Tamelokpo and Abdoulaye Mando

Introduction

This case study is about knowledge management in the integrated soil fertility management (ISFM) in the particular context of Togo. During the project a lot of experiences from the field of knowledge generation and sharing were accumulated by farmers and the International Center for Soil Fertility and Agricultural Development (IFDC) with its partners from the national agricultural research and extension system in Togo. This case study analyses the KM activities that support the ISFM project.

This case study first describes the context of soil fertility KM in southern Togo. Next, knowledge content is discussed, with a particular emphasis on the ISFM knowledge of various actors (external and local knowledge). Then KM activities are described, specifically the tools for sharing knowledge and the access to and use of ISFM knowledge by different actors, especially resource-poor farmers. Finally the constraints and opportunities for an effective KM strategy for ISFM are analysed and recommendations for a strategy towards better KM are provided.

4.1 Introducing adapted fertilization practices in Togo

Togo: a particular context

Togo is a country in West Africa. Its land area is 56,000 km^2 and its population is estimated to be more than 5 million inhabitants. Poverty is unequally distributed across the country, and is more widespread in rural areas. As almost 80% of the poor are farmers, improving the rural poor's livelihoods depends on ensuring their access to potentially productive land and relevant knowledge. However, demographic pressure and the predominant farming practices result in land scarcity and considerable environmental degradation. Although the government has voiced its intention to support private producers, the potential of the agricultural sector is far from being realized. Farmers' concerns include: weak extension services, irrelevant agricultural research, unfavourable terms of trade, uncertain land tenure, insufficient transport and storage infrastructure,

---

[9] IFDC would like to acknowledge IFAD since a part of the experiences reported upon in this paper were supported by a grant (IFDC-535).

problematic access to water and, in particular, insufficient access to credit and fertilizers (World Bank, 2003). The actual economic situation of Togo is characterized by the collapse of public expenditure in agriculture which has led to a situation where public agricultural organizations are not able to do what they need to do to support farmers.

The nature of the problem: soil fertility decline in southern Togo

Southern Togo, located in the Maritime region, represents 11% of the total land area of Togo. It is the most populous zone of Togo, with a population density of 200 inhabitants per km^2 while the national average is 98 inhabitants per km^2. The climate is subequatorial with two rainy seasons, from April to July and from September to November. The average annual rainfall is between 900 and 1200 mm. The soils are very poor. Brabant et al. (1996) conducted a study on the status of the lands in Togo and found that high-level land degradation is happening primarily in southern Togo. Soil nutrient depletion in this area is principally caused by successive and continuous use of land. This situation has led to decreasing chemical soil fertility and a diminishing organic matter content of around 1%. Maize grain yields under local practices and without external inputs ranged from a widely variable 300 kg/ha to 700 kg/ha. In addition, the cassava starch factory in Ganavè, Southern Togo, has caused continuous cassava monoculture and subsequent soil depletion.

An ISFM project to address soil fertility decline problems in southern Togo

The ISFM project began in 1997 and is being implemented in seven countries in West Africa (Benin, Burkina Faso, Ghana, Mali, Niger, Nigeria and Togo). This case study will focus on Togo. The ISFM project addresses the soil resource base for intensive agriculture. The main focus is the promotion of soil fertility restoration and improvement to increase the efficiency of agricultural inputs. ISFM targets the improvement of (i) the soil organic matter quality status as well as quantity through crop residue recycling, (green) manure and compost application, agro-forestry, etc.; (ii) the phosphorus status (applications of phosphate rock, mineral fertilizers-P), and (iii) the pH of the soil. The promotion of soil fertility maintenance methods at more intensive levels of agricultural production is based on a combination of mineral and organic fertilization (Maatman et al., 2001; IFDC & TSBF-CIAT, 2005). Complementary methods to increase productivity of land, labour and capital are also promoted, for example soil and water conservation methods, improved seeds, and machinery.

The 'soft' content of the ISFM project is support to rural organizations and institution building in order to improve farmers' access to external inputs and to strengthen their role with regards to decision-makers. A key emphasis was put on the development of both local and regional products, factors (including credits) and markets (for example through training and networking with traders (input-dealers), transporters and other actual and potential private-sector actors). The ISFM concept defined in this way broadens the field of analysis, taking into consideration nutrient management, soil and water conservation in particular ecosystem like watershed, water management in irrigated systems, germplasm, and plant genetic resources (improved and local seeds).

4.2 Knowledge content: how to maintain soil fertility under more intensive cultivation

Three types of knowledge on soil fertility maintenance are discussed hereunder: local knowledge about soil fertility maintenance, interventionists' knowledge about ISFM and socially constructed knowledge.

Local knowledge about soil fertility maintenance

In the different ecological zones and production systems in southern Togo farmers have developed – both empirically and through their daily activities – enormous experience and innovative practices regarding the management of their soil. In the three ecological zones studied, farmers distinguished different types of soils depending on colour and texture. They are aware that the soil contains some 'vitamins' (soil nutrients) that are necessary for crop growth and better yields.

The different types of soils distinguished by farmers in the maize-cassava zone are: *kodjin* for red ferralitic soils, *bakomê* for black soils and *bado* for heavy clay soils. In the irrigated scheme of the Zio valley, farmers distinguish between loamy and clay soils. Each type of soil was differently managed by those farmers. Sandy soils are quickly depleted compared to the clay soils. Farmers have their own indicators for soil fertility. The presence of some plants is an indication that the soils are fertile. For instance farmers in Djaka Kopé explained that *hadougogo (Commelina benghalensis)*, and *anouto (Blactuca taraxacifolia)* plants both indicate that the soil is fertile. An infestation of *dou (Striga hermontica)* on a plot and the presence of *agbenomakoui (Commelina forskalei)* indicate poor soils. Farmers adapted the crops to the characteristics of their soils, as an old farmer in Souzakopé explains:

> *"Before, farmers did not use fertilizers and they adapted the crops to different types of soils. Pepper crops do not perform very well on sandy soils. Cassava improves the structure of the soil for maize cultivation."*

Farmers have developed different ways to improve their soils. They believe organic matter *(zouko)* **to be** a key element, and so brought organic waste to their farms. In the maize-cotton zone, farmers practiced a relay cropping system where maize is first sown in March and April, and when it is at the flowering and maturation stage cotton is sown in the furrows of maize plants. When the maize is harvested all the maize straw is recycled under the cotton plants to add organic matter to the soil.

In the irrigated rice zone, farmers argued that there is a relationship between the nature of the soil and the quality of the rice they produce. Farmers explained that healthy soils with a very good nutrient content will produce good quality rice. According to the farmers, poor water management in the irrigated plots would affect the quality of rice after harvesting and processing. Poor drainage, resulting in inundation and mud in the irrigated plots during the maturation period of paddy rice, will make the husk very dirty. Some grains in the mud will start germinating before the harvest.

Interventionists' knowledge about ISFM

IFDC and its partners ITRA and ICAT have developed fertilizer recommendations for irrigated rice systems to improve the fertility of the soils and rice productivity. On-farm experiments have revealed that returning rice straw to the soil in irrigated schemes helped improve the organic matter content of soil. The recommendations varied according to the type of soil (see Box 6). The use of Togolese rock phosphate is also promoted.

In the maize-cotton system, farmers applied fertilizers to cotton based on national recommendations. After the cotton is harvested, maize is grown without applying fertilizers but it was observed that the leaves yellowed during the flowering period. IFDC and its partners ITRA and ICAT have developed, with farmers, two options to respond to nutrient deficiency in maize in this zone (see Box 6). Researchers have introduced soybean into the maize-cotton system to improve the organic matter content of the soil. The idea was to cultivate during year one and recycle the crop residues, and during year two maize and cotton would be grown using the fertilizer recommendations.

Box 6   ISFM options introduced by the interventions

Irrigated rice system
- Fertilizer recommendations per hectare when straw is recycled on a plot

On clay soil: 150 kg of NPK 15-15-15 + 100 kg of urea (46%)
On sandy soil: 300 kg of NPK 15-15-15 + 165 kg of urea (46%)
On loamy soil: 200 kg of NPK 15-15-15 + 200 kg of urea (46%)
- Fertilizer recommendations per hectare when straw is not recycled on a plot

On clay soil: 200 kg of NPK 15-15-15 + 100 kg of urea (46%)
On sandy soil: 400 kg of NPK 15-15-15 + 135 kg of urea (46%)
On loamy soil: 300 kg of NPK 15-15-15 + 167 kg of urea (46%)

Maize–cotton system
After the cultivation of cotton on which 150 kg of NKPSB 12-20-18-5-1 and 150 kg of urea (46%) were applied per hectare:
Minimum Option for maize: 100 kg of NPK 15-15-15 + 100 kg of urea (46%) per hectare
N Boost Option for maize: 100 kg of NPK 15-15-15 + 150 kg of urea (46%) per hectare
General Boost Option for maize: 200 kg of NPK 15-15-15 + 100 kg of urea (46%) per hectare

Maize–cassava system
Minimum Option: 150 kg of K2SO4 + 50 kg of urea (46%) + 300 kg of Togolese Rock Phosphate (TRP) per hectare
N Boost Option: 150 kg of K2SO4 + 100 kg of urea (46%) + 300 kg of TRP per hectare
General Boost Option: 200 kg of NPK 15-15-15 + 100 kg of urea (46%) per hectare

In the maize-cassava system, the innovation was the introduction of K-fertilizer (see Box 6). IFDC and ITRA have introduced Togolese rock phosphate to improve the soil, and recommend an application rate of 300 kg per ha for a period of three years.

Socially constructed forms of knowledge

An important body of knowledge that was identified at farmer level had resulted from their interaction with interventionists (researchers, extension staff and NGO professionals). Farmers generated new knowledge by adapting different ISFM options to their agro-ecological and socio-economic conditions. Figure 8 illustrates the process behind socially constructed knowledge. In the interface between farmers and interventionists, farmers in southern Togo critically selected and adapted external knowledge to their local conditions.

The ISFM option which was introduced into the irrigated rice zone comprised improved rice varieties (such as IR841, Bouaké189) and farmers were able to produce between 5 and 6 tons/ha of rice, when normally they had only produced between 1.5 and 4 tons/ha. Seed of the new varieties were continuously reproduced by farmers through

Figure 8 Socially constructed knowledge through interactions between the intervention's and the local knowledge

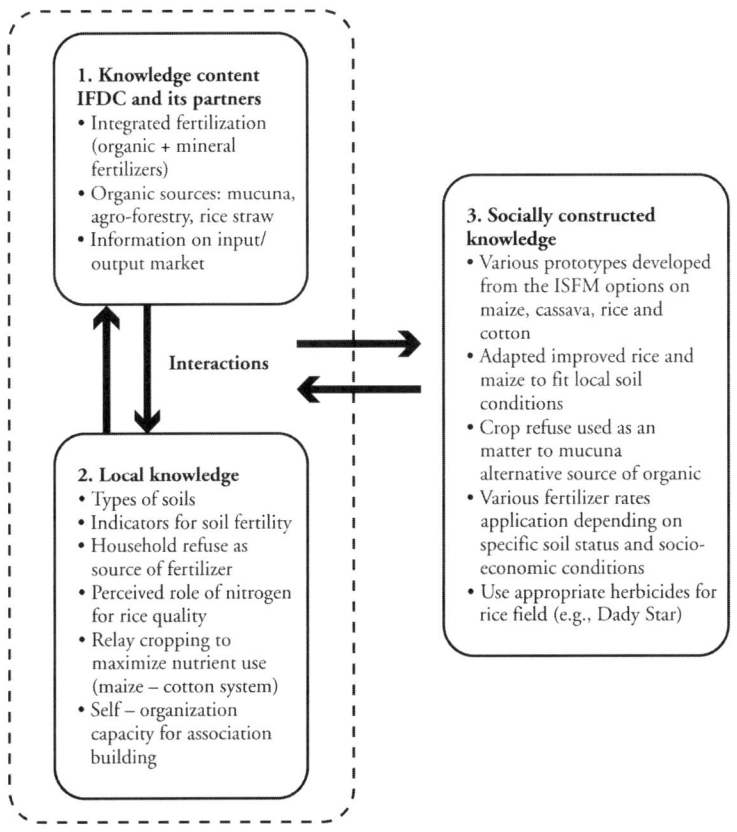

natural selection. The Ministry of Agriculture sent one farmer to Indonesia to learn from other farmers there. He returned with an early mature rice variety from Indonesia that could be cropped three times a year in the Zio Valley. The farmer then supplied friends and relatives with seed which they multiplied for wider distribution.

The ISFM project began with maize-mucuna-fertilizers options, and then interactive processes with farmers generated the idea of conducting participatory nutrient omission trials in maize-cassava cropping systems, taking into account the farmers' diverse agro-ecological and socioeconomic conditions. The discoveries made by male and female farmers themselves about potassium (K) deficiency for sustainable cassava production has led to a tremendous change.

Some farmers strategically hid their knowledge from others to gain a competitive advantage, as illustrated by the story of a farmer in Assomè:

> *"One of the farmers in Assomè had some problems with the herbicides he used. They were not effective in controlling the weeds in his rice field. One day he went to an input dealer who advised him to use a herbicide called DADY STAR. He used it in his rice field and the results were satisfactory. However, he decided to apply the herbicide early in the morning so that other people would not know what he was using. He thus hid his success from the other farmers, who wondered how he managed the weeds in his rice field so successfully. One day, he forgot an empty packet of DADY STAR near his rice field and a farmer saw it and ran off to buy some for himself. Now DADY STAR is widely used by the rice growers in the Zio valley irrigated scheme."*

4.3   Whose knowledge?

Besides the farmers, many organizations were involved in the ISFM project in southern Togo. The IFAD-funded (via a loan) Village Organization and Development Project (PODV) has previously played a key role in knowledge sharing among resource-poor farmers, mainly female farmers in the southern region of Togo. The following organizations were closely involved in the ISFM project implemented in southern Togo by IFDC:

- **IFDC-Africa Division**. IFDC, an international centre for soil fertility and agricultural development, is the main implementer of the ISFM project. . IFDC supports ISFM research and development activities in Togo to increase agricultural productivity and farmers' incomes by improving the natural resource base. The focus is on strengthening the capacity of farmers and other stakeholders through improved ISFM options and tools development in order to facilitate access to relevant knowledge, technologies, market information and policy instruments.
- **Institut Togolais de Recherche Agronomique (ITRA)** contributes to the ISFM project in southern Togo by facilitating joint-learning and participatory experiments with farmers. ITRA is the Togolese national research institute, and syntheses of innovations and technologies were transferred to the users through the national extension services (see next bullet point).
- **Institut de Conseil et d'Appui Techniqtie (ICAT)**, the national extension organization, has contributed through the ISFM project to the development or consolidation of professional agricultural organizations by helping and advising farmers to create

cooperatives and encouraging the development of unions or federations to enable farmers to increase their participation in agricultural policymaking.
- **DRAEP** supplied fertilizers to farmers involved in the ISFM project in southern Togo. The DRAEP is the regional office of the Secretariat General which is the permanent technical and administrative division of the Ministry of Agriculture, husbandry and fisheries. As a public organization, the **Secretariat General** has a mandate to develop national agricultural policy and an action plan through a participatory process, and to ensure the coordination, monitoring, and control of the implementation of agricultural policy. The Secretariat General supervises the programmes of central services, projects, public and semi-public services (for example ICAT and ITRA) and NGOs working in the agricultural sector.
- **NGOs** are directly or indirectly involved in the implementation of the ISFM project in southern Togo. The **Centre de Recherche et d'Essai des Modèles d'Autopromotion (CREMA)** is a local NGO which works in the maize-cassava and maize-cotton zone within the ISFM project. Professionals from this NGO are involved in community facilitation processes. The Programme de Développement Intégré de la Vallée de Zio (PADIV-Zio) is a consortium of five NGOs working in the irrigated rice area. They worked mainly on micro-finance issues to support rice farmers in the Zio valley.
- **Private companies and businesses** were not heavily involved in the ISFM project. Micro-financing structures like the **Coopérative d'Epargne et de Crédit (COPEC)** and Microfund provided credit to farmers but they did not support them in management skills. CALLI Togo, AGRI TOGO 2000, and CHIMAGRO are all companies that supplied pesticides and herbicides to farmers. Their fertilizer prices were not attractive to the farmers, who preferred the subsidized offer from DRAEP.
- **Farmer's associations and unions**. IFDC recently recorded 14 farmer's unions in southern Togo, each consisting of several village-level farmer's associations. The most active farmer's unions in the ISFM project are the GBENODOU in the maize-cassava zone and the Union Groupements de Producteur Agricole (UGPA) of AHEPE in the maize-cotton zone.

4.4 Knowledge management activities

A closer look at Figure 8 above shows that different types of knowledge can be distinguished and analysed: the interventionists' knowledge, local knowledge ('tacit knowledge') and an adapted body of socially constructed knowledge. The best ways to strengthen (manage) knowledge will depend on the type of knowledge to be strengthened. The KM activities implemented by the ISFM project can be categorized according to the type of knowledge (see Table 1).

Strengthening the interventionists' body of knowledge

These activities cover the ways the interventionists' knowledge was shared. The packaging of the knowledge is specific to researchers, extension staff, and NGO professionals. The tools that IFDC used to share this knowledge were training workshops, print materials and websites.

Table 1   Different types of knowledge and tools to manage them

Type of knowledge management	Tools for management	Scale of targeting	Characteristics
1. Strengthening the interventionist's body of knowledge	• Training • Print materials • Websites	• International and national actors (researchers, extension workers, NGOs, etc.)	• Focus on large audience • Knowledge format not necessarily accessible to actors such as farmers
2. Strengthening the local body of knowledge by creating opportunities for interaction	• Exchange visits • Study tours • Rural workshop • Rural radio	• Southern region of Togo • Other regions with similar agro-ecosystems • Neighbouring villages	• Stimulate farmer experiments and adaptation in many villages • Provide pathways to scale up adapted knowledge with groups of farmers
3. Strengthening the interaction between local and interventionists' knowledge	• Learning and Action Research (PLAR) processes • Activities like field school	• Groups of farmers willing to participate in experiential learning processes	• Capturing local knowledge through the process • Joint knowledge generation and sharing • Dynamic and potential to reshape intervention knowledge content

Training workshops

IFDC organizes international training workshops to share knowledge on fertility management with participants from international and national research and development organizations, universities, extension organizations, and government investment projects funded by organizations like the World Bank, IFAD, etc. Examples of such knowledge include principles of integrated fertilization, site-specific fertilizer recommendations depending on agro-ecological and socio-economic conditions, and using decision-support tools (such as QUEFT, DSSAT, and NUTMON).

Printed materials

The ISFM project involved several partners in different pilot learning sites in West Africa and there is a synthesis of the activities of all the different partners in an AISSA (Agricultural Intensification in Sub-Saharan Africa) tool box (Gross & Ezui, 2005).
A newsletter, *Faces of AISSA*, shares success stories from the ISFM project activities with farmer's associations, decision-makers, and donors. Experiences from other countries and shared through AISSA can be used in southern Togo. Field data are also published in international journals for a scientific audience.

Websites

To share the interventionists' knowledge, the AISSA network uses a website. The AISSA website (www.aissa.org) makes printed materials available electronically. Market information, promising commodities and value chains are shared via the Agri-Business Information Points (ABIP), which are linked to the agri-trade website (www.agritrade.biz).

The websites give research and development professionals working in southern Togo a chance to update their knowledge to effectively support farmers.

Strengthening the body of local knowledge

This type of KM activity focuses on farmers. It comprises:

Study tours and exchange visits
Study tours are organized for the farmers, with the participation of researchers and extension workers, in areas where particular options for ISFM had been developed and adapted by farmers for their agro-ecological and socio-economic conditions. Farmers are brought from different areas of Togo or from other countries in West Africa to discuss and learn from their fellow farmers what they have learned from the ISFM project. Exchange visits are systematically organized during the cropping seasons around farmer-led demonstration plots and jointly designed learning plots. In addition to members of the learning group, non-participating farmers in the village and farmers from the surrounding villages or other intervention areas are also invited.

A rural workshop
This activity involved several actors: farmers from different villages, farmer's associations and unions, local chiefs, representatives from the Ministry of Agriculture, directors of the research and extension institute, and rural development professionals. In many circumstances the ISFM options that had been jointly developed with farmers could have been used widely if some constraints had been addressed at decision-making level. For example, IFDC and its partners have used single fertilizers like K_2SO_4 (potassium) and Togolese rock phosphate to develop ISFM options in the maize-cassava zone (see Box 6 in Section 4.2). In Togo, only NPK 15-15-15 and urea are available in this area. The aim of the rural workshop was not only to share knowledge and information, but also to make decision-makers aware of the constraints that create barriers to the use of new knowledge.

A rural radio programme
A pilot rural radio programme was tested in southern Togo to encourage the exchange of knowledge and information among farmers about the outcomes of the ISFM project. The approach enabled farmers to pass their messages on to other farmers who were organized into listening groups. A particular emphasis was put on the knowledge that was internalized in some farmers' practices (such as the role of organic matter, mucuna, and household refuse) and that were likely to provide solutions for the farmers who were not already involved in the learning processes.

Strengthening interaction between local and interventionists' knowledge

Opportunities were create for interaction between the actors involved in the mutual learning processes in order to enable the adaptation of knowledge.

Participatory learning and action research
The actors' knowledge as synthesized in Figure 8 is dynamic. Actors adapt their knowledge when they work together. Participatory learning and action research (PLAR) was used in southern Togo for KM. It combined participatory diagnosis methods and the introduction of modules to facilitate knowledge generation, exchange and use. Participatory methods such as mapping village terroires, transect walks, resource flow mapping, and Venn diagramming were used to generate and share knowledge about local soil resources and cropping systems. The process is kept as flexible as possible to create a suitable environment for adult learning. Example of the modules include participatory observation of soils, fertilizer identification and design of diagnostic plots, and an introduction to maize and cassava plant-growth performance indicators.

4.5 Towards a KM approach: creating knowledge impact

Effective KM for soil fertility management requires a strong partnership of relevant actors who have a common desire to work in a synergistic manner. Previous sections outlined their different bodies of knowledge. Access to and use of soil fertility management knowledge by different actors is constrained by different factors, including the cognitive ability of the actors, their socio-economic conditions and the wider institutional and political situation in Togo. Different tools were used to manage knowledge within the ISFM project as groups of farmers worked towards improved land productivity and sustainable livelihoods. How can effective KM strategies be put in place to manage IFDC's activities, the diversity of the farmers' reality, their way of communicating, and the policy environment?

Actual use of knowledge

Use by farmers
Farmers learned from their own farming and natural resources management practices and from observation, experimentation and many other sources. This information was not documented. While the interventionists' knowledge (synthesized in Figure 8) is not easily accessible to farmers, there is a tendency for researchers to overlook or ignore information, outside the formal research-extension linkages. Mapping out all the sources of knowledge and linkages in the local context is very complex because there are so many different situations.

Farmers learned about soil fertility management from the learning groups of the ISFM projects in all three of the eco-zones in southern Togo. Fellow farmers learned how farmers who participated in the PLAR investigated their soil through participatory nutrient omission trials to discover for themselves what were the most appropriate fertilizers. They also learned about other types of fertilizers like K-fertilizer, Togolese rock phosphate, and other sources of organic matter like mucuna and household refuse. Some farmers in the Union des Groupements de Producteurs Agricole de Ahepe (UGPA) in the maize-cotton zone who had participated in the rural workshops organized by their fellow farmers in the maize-cassava zone were considered a source of knowledge in their area. The UGPA has played a crucial role in enabling resource-poor farmers to access knowledge on soil fertility management through such knowledge-sharing activities. Thus, knowledge management through interactions between interventionists and farmers (Type 2) and between the farmers themselves (Type 3) was very effective in enabling farmers to access new knowledge. This is confirmed by the analysis which fertility management practices were adopted in the three eco-zones the ISFM project worked in. Table 2 shows that most farmers adapted knowledge, and hence applied both forms of knowledge.

Table 2   Percentage of male and female farmers who adapted soil fertility management options in their cropping systems

Adaptation of soil fertility management options in cropping systems by farmers	Male farmers		Female farmers		Total	
	Count	%	Count	%	Count	%
Use of mucuna only	15	33	9	14	24	22
Use of household refuse only	3	7	5	8	8	7
Use of household refuse + mucuna	8	17	16	25	24	22
Use of all kinds of organic matter	1	2	2	3	3	3
Use of mucuna + mineral fertilizers (urea, NPK, potash)	3	7	5	8	8	7
Use of household refuse + mineral fertilizers (urea, NPK, potash)	2	4	4	6	6	6
Use of different sources of organic matter + fertilizers (urea, NPK, potash)	9	20	13	21	22	20
Rock phosphate + fertilizers (urea, NPK, potash)	5	11	9	14	14	13
Total	46		63		109	

Source: Akollor, 2008.

The use of available knowledge by farmers was critical in southern Togo since the majority of them were illiterate, especially the female farmers. A survey conducted in the maize-cassava zone on a sample of 63 women farmers revealed that 95% were illiterate (Akollor, 2007). A survey that estimated the investment capacity of farmers revealed that farmers do not have sufficient financial resources. This situation pushes farmer to use their socially constructed knowledge (see in Figure 8). Very few farmers can use the interventionists' knowledge.

Knowledge about marketing and information on the prices or value of their crops is not accessible to farmers (the trend observed in other countries of farmers in remote areas using mobile phones to access this information seems less common in Togo). Farmers asked their fellow farmers who had recently returned from cities like Lomé for the going price of maize. The president of the UGPA in the maize-cotton zone said that the best way to access knowledge was to set up a strong association to capitalise on opportunities for resource-poor farmers who would not be able to solve their problems alone. Such associations and unions should search for new knowledge and information and share it with the other members.

Use by researchers and agricultural extension workers
Strengthening the interventionists' knowledge (Type 1 KM activities) enabled many researchers from the national agricultural research and extension organization to

participate in national and international training programmes organized by IFDC. The project's research and development partners in southern Togo have access to new knowledge through their direct participation in the other types of Type 3 KM activities. It is questionable whether they are able to apply the things they learn, however, due to the actual political and socio-economic context of Togo.

Sustainable engagement of the knowledge users
All KM tools have their strengths and weaknesses. Some, like websites and print material, may help reach a larger audience but are difficult to maintain, as explained in Table 3. Others rely on the actors' motivation to take ownership from the ISFM project. It goes without saying that a KM strategy needs to use a combination of tools to reach different types of stakeholders and effectively generate and share knowledge on soil fertility management.

Constraints in the management of knowledge

The use of knowledge on soil fertility management described in Table 3 was subject to a number of limiting factors.

Diversity of the farmers' situations
The study was conducted in three zones with different cropping systems and farmer soil management practices for maize, cassava, cotton and rice. To be really useful a different combination of knowledge was required for each zone. For example, while fertilizer recommendations by the national extension services were the same for the whole country, farmers were experiencing different realities in the maize-cassava and maize-cotton zones. The national system (research and extension organizations, NGOs, private sector) covering KM on soil fertility was not able to cope with the diversity of farmers' situations.

Farmer access to KM services was also different. In the maize-cotton zone, for example, the Société Togolaise du Coton, the government cotton-promotion company, appointed a technician to help farmers in technical matters and commercial issues. In two other zones extension staff was assigned the responsibility of supporting farmers in this way but they did not have the budget to do their work.

Necessity of complementary knowledge
Not all the KM activities discussed above were integrated into a general KM strategy. For example, farmers in the study area were convinced that the ISFM project had resulted in an increase of their maize and cassava yields. But the same farmers complained that they could not sell their products. At the same time there are very interesting KM activities within other projects at IFDC, such as the facilitation of ABIP by using an agri-trade network to access market information. These activities could be linked to the ISFM farmers in southern Togo. A good KM strategy would include different types of knowledge, for example relevant soil fertility management options, market information, skills to manage farms to ensure a return on investments, and information on promising commodity value chains (adding value to their product through processing). Most activities are carried out through different projects and programmes, but they were not consolidated into an overall KM strategy.

Table 3   Knowledge management activities, target beneficiaries and sustainability issues

KM activities	For whom?	Sustainability issues
Websites (AISSA), Agribusiness Information Point (ABIP) linked to Agri-trade network	Integrated Soil Fertility Management (ISFM) project partners, researchers, extension workers, NGOs, traders and producers associations	The contribution of partners to the websites is not yet optimal because the websites are linked to projects and may not continue when projects end
• Print materials • AISSA tool box, Faces of AISSA • Scientific publications	ISFM project partners, researchers, extension workers, NGOs	This activity is linked to the project and may not continue when the project ends
Training workshops (international, regional, and national)	Participants from international organizations, universities, extension organizations, government investment projects funded by organizations like the World Bank, IFAD, partners of the ISFM project	The quality of the training attracted funds from the participants themselves. Sustainability depends on strategies to maintain good quality and standards for the training
Facilitation of PLAR processes	Farmers, farmer groups, researchers and extension workers	Depends on the motivation of partners to take the ownership of the process
Study tours (with farmers, researchers, extension workers)	Farmers, farmer groups, researchers and extension workers	Depends on the motivation of partners to take the ownership of the process
Exchange visits with farmers	Farmers, farmer groups	Depends on the motivation of partners to take the ownership of the process
Rural workshops	Farmers, farmer groups, researchers and extension workers, decision-makers local authorities, input dealers, traders	Depends on the motivation of partners to take the ownership of the process
Rural radio programmes	Farmers, farmer groups	Depends on the motivation of national rural radio programmes to take the ownership of the process

Effectiveness of communication among actors
A crucial condition for KM is that all the actors involved in the processes communicate effectively. Farmers did not understand the scientific representation of nitrogen (N), phosphorus (P) and potassium (K) used during the participatory experiment. In some communities, however, farmers could easily understand the role of nutrients when facilitators used 'vitamin' as a metaphor. In the maize-cassava zones, when mucuna was used as a relay crop with maize, the farmers lost the short rainy season but their soil was

improved for the next long season. Scientists working in the ISFM project have demonstrated that when farmers used the mucuna and fertilizers option, their subsequent maize yield was sufficiently higher to compensate for the loss of the short rainy season. However, farmers themselves incorporated into their analysis aspects of risk and uncertainty of rains that could cause crops to fail in the long rainy season and succeed in the short one. This was not known by the interventionists. Many KM strategies were not successful because the facilitators were not skilled enough to communicate effectively with farmers.

Institutional aspects of knowledge management

The present situation
Government organizations for agricultural research and development do not function in a way that could allow KM strategies to be effective. Due to the long and enduring political crisis and the withdrawal of development aid by the European Community (EC) and many other donors, there was no recent R&D funding for the public agricultural organization in the study area. Also the links between researchers and extension workers in Togo is very weak, so there were no existing strategic interfaces between them on soil fertility issues in the study areas. Extension workers received little training and were poorly equipped to respond to the various and diverse problems in the different ecological zones. Farmers who learned new practices did not then have access to external inputs (fertilizers, seeds). All actors, including those in the private sector, the NGOs and the universities did not work as 'system' that was responsive to a rapidly changing context.

Opportunities for a farmer-driven KM strategy: emergence of farmer's unions
The emergence of a farmer's union is a good opportunity to further develop and implement a systematic KM strategy for soil fertility management. A strong and internalized body human capital was built at farmer level by the farmers of the union GBENODOU, and they were convinced that they should start a process to scale up knowledge on soil fertility management. According to the president of the union:

> "It is not easy for farmers to find time and to go and teach other farmers what we have learned from the ISFM project. An alternative is to focus on the farmer's associations that are members of the union."

Farmers who participated in the PLAR processes on soil fertility management are willing to share the knowledge they have acquired. While in most circumstances individual farmers are competitors (see the example described earlier of the farmer hiding his use of DADY STAR herbicide), the GBENODOU union believes that they would not be able to seize various opportunities if they did not act collectively as a union and maintain strong forward and backward linkages that would enable them to negotiate at different levels for access to both inputs and markets. The GBENODOU perspective on knowledge sharing with fellow farmers who belong to the associations that are members of the union is as follows:

- First, it is important to know the members of the farmer's association that belong to the union. This is important because only representatives should attend meetings and the union does not always have a clear picture of what is going on in each farmer's association.

- Second, a learning process will be set up that includes all members of the farmer's association. As in the case of soil fertility management, the process starts with the discovery of different types of fertilizers and nutrients.
- Third, we design experiments to investigate our soils. What types of nutrients are missing in the soils? How do we combine different sources of mineral and organic fertilizers? What are the roles of different types of nutrients? We explain different sources of organic matter to farmers and how organic matter could improve productivity.
- Fourth, we involve many farmers in a learning process during the experimentation phase so that they learn by doing.

The GBENODOU union has selected two villages to implement this sequence.

Farmer-driven approaches can be good for achieving a common goal. Several functions or tasks involved in the implementation of a KM strategy could be shared between farmer's unions and the project staff. The union could organize KM activities such as exchange visits with farmers and then convey farmers' needs to policy level.

4.6   Conclusions

The KM for soil fertility management addressed in this case study is based on the IFDC's activities in collaboration with its national Togolese partners (ITRA, ICAT, NGOs). The analysis of KM processes for IFSM covered, but also stimulated, interaction between farmers' knowledge and the knowledge of the project staff, which led to socially constructed and adapted forms of knowledge by resource-poor farmers in southern Togo. Thanks to KM activities (training, print materials, rural workshops, exchange visits, PLAR, etc.) each farmer in the intervention areas has used – depending on his or her socioeconomic conditions – at least one component (e.g., mucuna, crop residues, household refuse, rock phosphate, urea, etc.) of the soil fertility management options that were developed.

A comprehensive national framework for effective KM strategies would support institutions and conducive policies. The sustainability of the KM activities depends on the potential of key Togolese actors such as farmers, researchers, extension agents, universities, local NGO professionals from agricultural investment projects to take ownership of these practices. But this process is constrained by the political, institutional and socio-economic situation in Togo. The emergence of farmer's unions in southern Togo, offers an opportunity for the development of a farmer-driven KM strategy, one that would scale up the soil-fertility management options developed to help resource-poor farmers to maintain the fertility of their soils.

5 Knowledge management for introducing soil and water conservation into the agricultural practices of the Mahi people in Benin

Constant Dangbégnon, Suzanne Nederlof, Mathias Ahounou and Gustave Kpagbin

Introduction

This case study is about knowledge management (KM) for natural resource use and environmental protection in Benin. The quality of the natural resource base determines the availability of foods and income in rural areas. There is an increased general recognition of the importance of knowledge as a key resource for the development of economies. This case study focuses on land resource management in the Commune of Ouèssè, in the Central region of Benin, and analyses how KM could enhance the integration of soil and water conservation into the agricultural practices of the Mahi people. In this commune the Mahi people used to practice shifting cultivation, which led to environmental degradation. Many attempts have been made to adapt the Mahi people's practices to the changing context of increased degradation.

The study describes the context of land resource management in watersheds in Ouèssè, then the knowledge about land resource management in watersheds of different actors is discussed. Next, we present the KM activities that were deliberately implemented to share knowledge amongst different actors, and finally we discuss the constraints and opportunities for a more deliberate KM strategy, and recommend ways forward.

5.1 From shifting cultivation to more permanent agriculture in Benin

Benin: a short history

Benin is a long narrow country in West Africa, covering an area of 112,622 km^2 and with a population of approximately 7 million people, 31% of whom live in urban areas. The population of Benin is concentrated in the south, and density varies widely, from over 300 inhabitants per km^2 in the south to less than 40 in the north. About 40% of the population lives in urban areas. In 1974, the government declared that Benin would adopt a socialist development model based on Marxist-Leninist principles. In 1989 the government was facing economic problems and abandoned its socialist path, conceding to multiparty elections in 1991. In 1993 the 'Projet de Restructuration des Services Agricoles' (PRSA) was implemented with the support of the World Bank. The main idea of this reform was to transfer commercial, production and industrial activities to the private sector, including farmer organizations, and to refocus the mandate of the national extension organization, CARDER, and the Ministry of Agriculture on public services while reducing their operational costs (World Bank, 2003). At the level of the Ministry of Agriculture, a directorate, the DIFOV *(Direction de la Formation Opérationnelle et de la Vulgarisation)*, was set up to design the national strategies for training and extension activities in Benin. The PRSA ended in 1998 but the agricultural organizations were not performing satisfactorily (World Bank, 2003: 3). The problems were related to the lack of human and financial resources. In response the government created two new organizations: at the regional level the *Centre Régional de Promotion Agricole* (CeRPA) and at the commune level the *Centre Communal de Promotion Agricole* (CeCPA). The new extension approach is based on 'advice' to farmers *(conseil agricole)*. DIFOV became the *Direction du Conseil Agricole et de la Formation Opérationnelle* (DICAF).

The nature of the problem: shifting cultivation leading to environmental degradation

Ouèsse is inhabited by the Mahi, who are one of the major ethnic groups in this region and are farmers. Rural population density is low. Traditionally they practice shifting cultivation, clearing land in the *agbovê*; the *agbovê* is in fact a very old fallow and thus fertile land that did not need to be fertilized. The use of *agbovê* is based on *houinnou* which means the 'front of the furrows': when a Mahi farmer orients his *houinnou* in one direction, he owns of all the space ahead his *houinnou* until he meets with an obstacle like a river or a hill. The farms in the *agbovê* are far from the village (sometimes 15 kilometres away). Mahi farmers build small houses *(glécohoué)* and live there during the cultivation period.

As population density increases the system becomes less stable. Farmers have to travel further to find new fertile land that has been sufficiently long under fallow. This causes family problems, as farmers cannot continue to live in the *glécohoué* when it cannot be reached in an hour or two. This means that farmers tend to return to nearby land before it has completely regenerated, which leads to low yields. The high proportion of short-term fallow land used also causes firewood scarcity and severe erosion (Dangbégnon et al., 2001). In 1997, the young farmers in the village particularly regretted that their parents had not invested more in the land around the village, for example by planting cashew trees.

Considering this problematic situation, the 'Direction des Forêts et Ressources Naturelles' (DFRN), through the 'Projet de Gestion des Ressources Naturelles' (PGRN) carried out by the 'Groupe d'Expertise et d'Ingenierie Rurale pour l'Auto-promotion du Monde Paysan' (GERAM) addressed watershed development issues that required a radical adaptation of the Mahi farmers' cultivation styles. Would the Mahi people be willing to invest in an agricultural plot of land for watershed development and abandon their shifting cultivation in the *agbovê*?

Projects for soil and water conservation in watersheds

The DFRN intervention focused on environmental concerns, particularly soil and water conservation through contour farming, tree planting and land registration. In addition Mahi farmers worked with researchers from INRAB (Institut National des Recherches Agricoles du Bénin) to address soil fertility issues, emphasising the improvement of the organic matter content of soils that had been degraded by severe erosion. INRAB's research and development (R&D) team was involved in on-farm technology development. Recently they and IFDC collaborated to introduce integrated soil fertility management (ISFM), which is based on a combination of mineral and organic fertilization. Complementary methods to increase land, labor and capital productivity are promoted, such as soil and water conservation improved seeds and machinery. In the Commune of Ouèssè, ISFM activities focused particularly on the efficient use of mineral fertilizers. INRAB's results on organic fertilizers are integrated into the ISFM options being developed by IFDC, for example on-farm experiments are conducted on plots that have been treated by *mucuna* or *aeschynomenea* through the INRAB work.

5.2 Knowledge content: soil and water conservation in Ouèssè

Different actors know different things about soil and water conservation in watersheds in Ouèssè. First the Mahi farmers' knowledge is discussed, then that of the main interventionists (DFRN and GERAM, INRAB and IFDC), and finally the socially constructed bodies of knowledge, that is knowledge that emerged from interactions between actors and a subsequent convergence of local and interventionist knowledge.

Mahi farmers' knowledge on soil fertility maintenance

Mahi people in Ouèssè have their own classification systems for soils. According to Mahi farmers, hydromorphic soils are found in the watershed lowlands or on the banks of seasonal or temporary rivers. They are very fertile. Upstream areas in watersheds are called *kpodji*, while *todo* are downstream. The sloping ground between upstream and downstream is called *todohoiun*, the direction of the watercourse. Micro-watersheds are called *saagodji*. A decrease in yield indicates poor soil according to Mahi farmers. They traditionally used *Cajanus cajan* fallow to improve the fertility of the soils. Grain legumes such as groundnuts and cowpea are cultivated when the soils were becoming less fertile. Fertilizers are used by farmers who cultivated cotton. Maize was rotated with cotton so that the residual effects of fertilizers would benefit maize crops.

Mahi farmers also have their endogenous way of controlling soil erosion in watershed ecosystems. Ridging before sowing crops such as maize, groundnut, cassava or yam is a common practice, as a farmer from *Gbanlin* explains:

> *In the past, our grandfathers used to practise tillage which consisted of making ridges parallel to the watercourse (called* todohoiun*). When they made the ridges perpendicular to the* todohouin*, runoff flew down the crops and the ridges. This caused serious damage to the farms. For that reason, our grandfathers were right to make their ridges parallel to the* todohouin*. Then the water flows in the furrows and cannot easily transport crops. An*

interesting thing is that the seeds of the weeds in the furrows are transported and hence one economizes on labour for weeding.

The farmers have also developed a body of knowledge to cope with the multidimensional nature of environmental problems that they are very aware of, mentioning the following consequences:
- The water in the wells and rivers is drying up.
- There is a scarcity of firewood compared to the past.
- There is water run-off and land degradation in the farmlands.
- Agricultural plots are now very far from the villages (the farmers have to travel far to find fertile land).

Interventionists' knowledge about soil fertility maintenance

DFRN and GERAM-NGO

DFRN and GERAM mobilized knowledge about how to restore ecological services in the watershed ecosystems degraded by Mahi farmers. Ecological services in this case are the functions performed by trees (vegetation cover) in regulating run-off and recharging water to prevent a quick drying-up of the rivers embedded in the watershed ecosystems.

Contour farming was proposed as an innovation to improve the farmlands in the watersheds. This technique consists of finding the contour lines in the watershed and ploughing the furrows along them. Vetiver grass is planted on these ridges in the contour lines. This technique was expected to halt run-off and provide better water infiltration water. Constructing ridges along the contour lines conserved water for the plants.

Other options to reverse the negative environmental degradation trends include tree planting and forestation. Water-control techniques such as check dams and silt traps, gully control structures, grassing artificial waterways, and planting vegetative barriers on contour lines are also promoted. Land-surveying activities are an important dimension of watershed development, as land tenure secures farmers investments.

INRAB

INRAB's knowledge in the watershed development process in the Commune of Ouèssè concerned the different sources of organic matter for soil fertility management. Alternative options for shifting cultivation were developed using cover crops such as *mucuna*, *aeschynomene* and *stylosanthes* to sustainably improve soil fertility and crop yields (Amadji et al., 2004a; 2004b; and 2005). The results in Table 4 show the benefits that can be obtained from yam production in two systems: the *agbovè* system (natural fallow) and using *gliricidia* and *aeschynomenea* covercrops. Although the latter system provides higher benefits, the *agbovè* system is still competitive enough (has a high enough yield) to attract farmers.

Brochures are produced in the local languages *(fon, nago)* to facilitate the use of these technologies by farmers. Agroforestry options based on gliricidia, acacia and moringa were also introduced. Gliricidia was used particularly for sedentary yam production system, as opposed to the traditional system based on shifting cultivation.

Table 4 Comparison of yam production benefits in the *gliricidia* and *aeschynomene* cover crops versus the natural fallow *(agbovê)* system

	Gliricidia and *aeschynomene*	*Agbovê* system: natural fallow (land clearing and burning)
Yam production (in tons/ha)	23	25
Aeschynomene seed production (in tons/ha)	0.26	-
Value of production (in FCFA)	1,420,000	1,280,000
Labour (person days/ha)	175	206
Production cost (in FCFA)	554,000	585,000
Benefits (in FCFA)	866,000	695,000

Source: Adapted from Amadji et al., 2007.

IFDC

IFDC's knowledge focuses on soil fertility and covers integrated mineral and organic fertilization of the maize cassava system. The search for an appropriate recommendation started with a participatory nutrient omission trial (PNOT) with farmers (see Box 7). As explained above, INRAB's knowledge about organic fertilizers was used.

Box 7 Specifics of the participatory nutrient omission trial (PNOT)

Content of PNOT for maize

T0 control	=	N0	P0	K0
T1	=	N90	P40	K50
T2	=	N0	P40	K50
T3	=	N90	P0	K50
T4	=	N90	P40	K0

Content of PNOT for cassava

T0 (control)	=	N0	P0	K0
T1	=	N60	P30	K100
T2	=	N0	P30	K100
T3	=	N60	P0	K100
T4	=	N60	P30	K0

Socially constructed forms of knowledge

Interactions based on knowledge from DFRN/GERAM, INRAB, IFDC and the Mahi farmers led to a socially constructed form of knowledge by those farmers.

Mahi farmers constructed 'meaning' through interaction with the interventionists in their area. For instance the local term *sedoku* (which means 'our common wealth from nature') was used to facilitate environmental awareness-raising among farmers. This concept captures in Mahi language the sustainability issue of natural resources use. Natural resources are perceived as the 'wealth' of present and future generations. Mahi farmers adapted their cultivation styles through joint learning processes with PGRN by introducing cover crops into their farming systems. They used the options proposed by INRAB where there was a market for the cover crops' seeds.

Figure 9 Socially constructed knowledge of Mahi farmers, gained through interactions with other actors

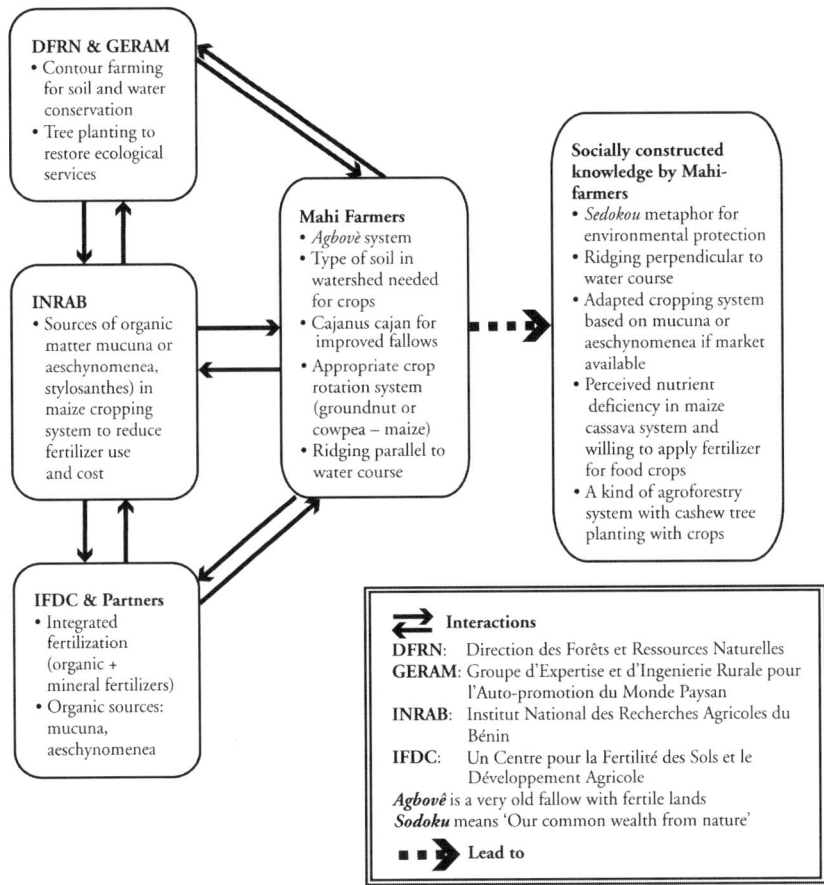

Through interaction with PGRN the farmers learned that contour farming could contribute to soil and water conservation. Many farmers chose to plant cashew trees on the contour lines to reduce erosion (rather than the vetiver grass introduced by PGRN) because of the growing economic value of cashew nuts.

Through interactive learning processes with PGRN (for example the participatory nutrient omission trials), farmers from Ouèssè also discovered that their soils require nitrogen (N) and phosphorus (P) to achieve better yields for maize and cassava cultivation. Some explained that they knew they needed to add nutrients to their soils but that fertilizers just were not available.

5.3 Whose knowledge?

Many actors were involved in KM on NRM in watersheds in the Commune of Ouèssè, central Benin. Their roles depended on the ways they perceived the nature of their problems. They are briefly described below:

- **The Mahi farmers** are one of the major ethnic groups in central Benin. Initial they were a group of small communities with diverse origins, brought together during the 17th to the 19th century by their joint resistance of the Abomey kingdom. During the French colonial era the Mahi people adopted this name despite their widely diverse origins. Out of a common experience that lasted more than two centuries (their painful dealings with Abomey), a social and ethnic identity arose. The Mahi farmers are well aware of the environmental degradation problems, but although the PGRN gave them an opportunity to improve their livelihoods, they faced a dilemma: should they continue with the *agbovè* system they knew or practice intensified agriculture and invest in their land? This critical question was the raison-d'être of the integrated interventions that aimed to develop knowledge to encourage the Mahi farmers to change their behaviour given the current circumstances.
- **DFRN (Direction des Forêts et Ressources naturelles)** is a department of the Ministry of Environment in Benin. Its main concern is the effective management of natural resources through the implementation of a project called PGRN. The ultimate aim of this project is to reverse land degradation in Ouèssè, which has decreased the productivity of agro-sylvo-pastoral ecosystems (Djohossou, 1993). Their general intervention objective was to support village communities to sustainably manage their natural resources in order to reinforce their capacity to manage their own development.
- **GERAM** (an NGO) was contracted by the PGRN. The view of the GERAM team is that the environmental degradation is caused by the agbovê system. Their main challenge is to design an appropriate intervention approach (including KM) that will stop the severe soil erosion problems.
- **CeRPA** is the main government centre for extension and rural development. It had only an indirect role in the execution of the PGRN by GERAM because of its known top-down approach and tendency to focus mainly on cotton production as promoted by the government (Dangbégnon, 1994). However at national level CeRPA's influence was felt through the national directorate in charge of rural extension, (actually the DICAV), which develops national policies and strategies for all actors involved in extension.
- **INRAB**, the Beninese national research service, conducts scientific research on problems that affect farmers in the different agro-ecological zones of the country. The PGRN was an opportunity for INRAB, through its R&D team, to synthesise existing innovations and technologies and help DFRN reverse the environmental degradation caused by the Mahi farmers. Participatory processes and on-farm experiments tested the various organic fertilizers that could improve the status of the soils that had been degraded by run-off (erosion).
- **IFDC** is an international centre for soil fertility and agricultural development. Their focus is on strengthening the capacity of farmers and other actors through improved ISFM options and tools development, and to facilitate access to relevant knowledge, technologies, market information and policy instruments. IFDC, in collaboration with the R&D team of INRAB, introduced integrated soil fertility management (ISFM), which is based on a combination of mineral and organic fertilizers. INRAB's results with organic fertilizers are integrated into the ISFM options being developed by IFDC at the Ouèssè pilot site.

5.4 Knowledge management activities

Each organization's knowledge addressed a particular problem related to soil fertility maintenance. Depending on the contribution of a specific nature of knowledge, the scale of intervention, KM activities were implemented as Table 5 shows.

Table 5 Different sources of knowledge and their contribution to soil fertility maintenance

Knowledge source	Contribution to soil fertility maintenance	Tools for management	Scale of intervention	Characteristics of the tool
DRFN/ GERAM (environmental issues)	• Restoration of ecological functions • Soil and water conservation	• Cultural events and folk media • Rural radio programme	• Commune of Ouèssè	• Large audience and high distortion of message
INRAB (soil organic matter status)	• Improvement of organic matter in watershed ecosystem	• Exchange visits • Farmer days • Print materials	• Neighbouring villages • School and church organizations in the Commune	• Stimulate farmer experimentation and adaptation • Provide pathways for scaling up
IFDC (integrated nutrient management)	• Improvement of integrated nutrient management	• Training • Participatory Learning and Action Research (PLAR)	• Groups of farmers willing to participate in PLAR processes	• Capturing local knowledge through the process • Joint knowledge generation and sharing
Mahi farmers (putting the 'whole' together)	• Adaptations and development of different prototypes	• Records on informal farmer-to-farmer communication	• Neighbouring villages	• No documentation

Knowledge management by DRFN/GERAM

Cultural events and folk media
Cultural events were organized and folk media, especially local singers and folklore groups, were used. Local singers were asked to chant a song that would raise interest in environmental management. Competitions among different folklore groups were organized, and judged based on the way they transmitted messages concerning watershed development. Folk media tend to stimulate quick mobilization.

Rural radio programmes
Mahi farmers consider rural radio a powerful means of communication and use it for announcing burial ceremonies, for example, to quickly inform people in the region. Rural radio was used by the GERAM team to broadcast programmes on a number of topics, including:
- the importance of contour farming for erosion control;
- land clearing and its consequences in the Commune of Ouèssè;
- opportunities for tree planting in the Commune of Ouèssè; and
- *sedoku*: safeguarding natural resources for future generations.

Through the use of rural radio the broadcasters were themselves given a voice to pass the message on environmental issues to the other Mahi farmers in the Commune of Ouèssè.

Training
Training in skills development enabled new local 'professionals' to emerge (for example nurserymen and beekeepers in gallery forests). By training locals the GERAM team transferred technical competencies to stakeholders, pooling many watershed development activities into the training sessions (such as setting contour lines, forestation techniques, and maintenance techniques).

Knowledge management by INRAB

Exchange visits and 'Farmer days' to share knowledge and experiences
INRAB organized exchange visits during the cropping seasons around on-farm experimentation plots. In addition to the learning group, non-participating farmers in the village and farmers from the surrounding villages were invited. Experience revealed that these activities were particularly useful when farmers themselves explained to others what they had been doing, showing the inputs they used and synthesising what they have learned to their fellows. Farmer days are organized when there are concrete results to share with participating and non-participating farmers. Extension workers, leaders of farmer organizations, the major of the Commune, and members of the local council are also invited to appreciate the contribution of research to improving agricultural productivity and farmer livelihoods.

Using print materials to share knowledge and information
INRAB designed print materials on *mucuna*, *aeschynomene*, and *stylosanthes* to synthesise knowledge and information concerning different sources of organic matter to improve crops yield. The print materials are presented in the local languages. Print materials on integrated nutrient management options were distributed to partners involved in the activities in Ouèssè. These materials are synthesised in the *Agricultural Intensification in Sub-Saharan Africa (AISSA) Tool Box* (Gross and Ezui, 2005). The strategy behind the AISSA toolbox is to share experiences on integrated nutrient management from other countries to support KM activities in the Commune of Ouèssè.

Knowledge management by IFDC

PLAR – Participatory Learning and Action Research
KM activities on integrated nutrient management create an opportunity for social interactions among the actors involved in mutual learning processes. Participatory learning and action research (PLAR) combined participatory diagnosis methods and modules to facilitate knowledge generation, exchange and use. Approaches such as Farmer Field Schools were used as adult education tools that aimed to expose farmers to a learning path in which they were gradually presented with new technologies, new ideas, new situations and new ways of responding to problems (FAO, 2000). The main objective was to increase farmers' capacity to respond adequately to changing farming situations.

Knowledge management by farmers

KM activities by farmers have only been recorded informally. No reporting is available at moment.

5.5 Towards a KM approach: creating knowledge impact

The KM activities described above were intended to facilitate access to and use of knowledge and information by the various actors directly or indirectly involved in the project. Access to knowledge by the actors (Mahi farmers, extension workers and researchers) depends both on the effectiveness of the mechanism being used to share knowledge and information flows and on participants' understanding of what is transmitted. The constraints and options of a KM approach are presented here, based on the foregoing analysis of KM activities, but also based on an analysis of the current use of this knowledge.

Actual use of knowledge by Mahi farmers

Discussions with Mahi farmers revealed that they obtained most of their information through cultural events, folk media, and rural radio programmes. The information from these media was mostly based on local perceptions, wisdom and cultural values. Farmers learned about new agricultural practices (new varieties, cultivation of new crops, soil and water conservation measures, etc.) from the members of learning groups established by the integrated project in the Commune of Ouèssè. For example, a farmer got information about using only appropriate soils for cassava cultivation from a fellow farmer. The farmer who passed the information got it during the PLAR process from a soil scientist who was doing land surveys in the area. The soil scientist observed during this process that the soils at the bottom of the watershed are too damp to produce cassava.

On-farm experiments conducted by INRAB's researchers and farmers stimulated informal knowledge and information sharing processes among farmers. Farmers obtained information that they used on their *terroir* through direct observations of other farms. For example, a farmer in Ouèssè noticed that other farmers had begun to diversify their cropping systems by growing rice. The farmer was enthused by this, and contacted the rice farmer to learn more about the practices involved and benefits that could be obtained from growing rice. The farmers who were not involved in farmer trials observed the experimental plots and asked the participating farmers what they were doing. We can safely assume, therefore, that everybody knows what is going on in the area, but solving problems is about using available knowledge to reverse environmental degradation.

Farmers faced dilemmas, and had to choose between investing in contour farming for soil and water conservation or continuing to clear land in the *agbovè*, which now knew would degrade the environment. Despite the risks of cultivating in the *agbovè* (including loss of life when people drowned crossing rivers), many farmers did not change their behavior. Some farmers explained that contour farming practices are expensive. A minimum of CFA F40,000 per hectare was required to adopt it. Others reported that the practice was time consuming for individuals. Farmers like having *mucuna* and *aeschynomenea* in their farming system because it improved the fertility of the soil. Even though these cover crops did not provide food, some farmers used them to suppress weeds. Some adopted *mucuna* and *aeschynomenea* because INRAB both brought the seeds and bought the ensuing crop, thus turning it into cash crops. However, these same farmers abandoned the practice when the researcher did not buy the seeds anymore.

The PLAR processes conducted with Mahi farmers enabled the researchers to discover nutrient deficiency in the soil (P, N and K in decreasing order of scarcity). However farmers complained that fertilizers were not available, especially simple fertilizers like P-fertilizers and K-fertilizers.

Among the adapted bodies of knowledge, ridging perpendicular to water courses is a practice which is internalized and widely used by Mahi farmers. As a farmer from Gbanlin explained:

> *'I was not a member of the group of farmers who worked with the PGRN on these issues (contour farming). Yet we all learned from those who did to ridge perpendicular to the water course. You can ask the question of anybody else in this village, you will hear the same story. It is a good practice compared to what our ancestors were doing. Our children will certainly do the same ....'*

Pioneer farmers in contour farming activities have introduced an agroforestry-like system by planting cashew trees on contour lines. The dissemination of this practice in the Commune of Ouèssè was accelerated by the growing market for cashew nuts during the 2000s in Benin.

Use by researchers and agricultural extension people

Many researchers from INRAB and the national extension organization who were working in the intervention area had access to knowledge on integrated nutrient management using decision-support tools (named NUTMON and DSSAT). The extension workers in the Commune of Ouèssè had access to knowledge through their participation in the different activities carried out by the INRAB researchers, including exchange visits and farmer days. Research findings were also synthesized, published and sold. However, extension workers did not buy these materials to support their activities with farmers, partly because they did not know about them and partly because most of them do not have the money. The link between researchers and extension workers is weak and does not lead to increased use of researcher knowledge by extension workers.

Institutional aspects of knowledge management

Questioning the effectiveness of the KM strategies put in place in Benin
Any KM strategy at local level, like that at the Commune of Ouèssè, depends on the institutional arrangements made at a higher level (ministries) to support knowledge generation and sharing. In Benin, the government attempted to design KM strategies at the start of the democratization process when investments in agriculture were made through the World Bank. Currently, the National Agricultural Extension System (NAES) – and more recently the Conseil Agricole (CA), a system based on management advice for family farms – is being implemented. These extension systems, developed by the Ministry of Agriculture, provide (on paper at least) ideas and perspectives for generating knowledge by different actors, tools for sharing the knowledge, and different levels of activities to improve farmer livelihoods. However, the major question is how effective are these KM strategies, which were put in place by the government to enable the sustainability of ongoing KM processes through the integrated project in the Commune of Ouèssè?

KM strategies based on the NAES appear to build on a pre-determined set of actors with whom knowledge is developed through pre-extension activities with farmers. Such a model has some limitations and cannot be used to cope with the issues in the Commune of Ouèssè. The actors involved in this knowledge process should rather be influenced by negotiation and mutual learning to change their behaviour regarding the management of watershed resources. Farmers in the intervention area are more likely to seek information, learn new skills and change their behavior when critical soil fertility problems make sense to them and to their daily lives (Dangbégnon, 1999: 26). In the NAES, KM activities such as information sharing, training and demonstrations are too limited and do not take into consideration local ways of communicating (metaphors, symbols and iconography for visual tools). The KM activities do not provide farmers with analytical tools the way a PLAR process does (described above), and which empower them to continuously respond to evolving conditions in their farms and the wider socio-economic environment.

The NAES KM system was recently assessed. Results revealed that the system performed poorly, and as a result a new approach has been developed, with the emphasis on introducing management advice for farmers: it is called 'Conseil Agricole' (CA).

The strong point of the CA approach is that the nature of the knowledge introduced to farmers is diversified, ranging from technical to socio-economic and institutional types of knowledge. Through this approach professionals at the ministry intend to add other issues to their KM strategy to compensate for some of the weaknesses in the NAES. The CA involves:
- tools for decision-making about family farm management;
- skills to analyse the economic returns of the farmers' activities;
- forecast tools for farmers;
- skills to enable farmers' organizations to design projects for funding; and

- skills to enable farmers to marketing their produce better and to negotiate better sales agreements.

Using CA is more demanding of human resources, however. The knowledge and skills required to do this type of work do not exist in the Commune. In addition, these new types of extension tools require an attitude change, which is not obvious for extension workers. Institutional and organizational management arrangements at the national and regional levels are top-heavy, while field staff are not available to implement the approach. Thus, the CA method is not yet working for the Mahi farmers in Ouèsse.

Towards decentralized KM strategies for soil fertility maintenance
What are the alternatives to improve the KM strategies put in place by the government in Benin?

First, the success of the IFDC programme was closely related to the effectiveness of communication with farmers using symbols and conventions developed together. Effective communication is the basis of any KM strategy.

Furthermore, initiating a dynamic learning system requires that the main themes are shared and endorsed at the Commune level. To achieve this it is vital to have decentralized public research and extension activities cooperating closely with NGOs and other actors in the area. Innovation strategies should stimulate participation. The private sector and the universities in particular are not yet strongly integrated into the innovation 'system', and so are not responsive to a rapidly changing context. For example, how can the input dealers facilitate access to external inputs (fertilizers, seeds) for farmers in the Commune of Ouèssè?

There is also an urgent need to rethink the KM strategies put in place by the Ministry of Agriculture in Benin, taking into consideration the decentralization process. Each Commune in Benin has a local parliament, a strategic development plan *(Plan de Développement Communal)*, and administrative units in charge of local development activities. These new actors from the Communes should play a key role in KM strategies. For example:
- The physical planning of the Commune area *(terroir)* to prevent ecosystem degradation can be addressed by the new Commune local government, together with the decentralized national research and development organizations. In addition to the previously mentioned KM activities that were aimed at raising awareness, the creation of coalitions involving political leaders, professionals and farmers is necessary to catalyse better soil fertility maintenance in the Commune of Ouèssè.
- KM activities such as cultural events and folk media, rural radio programmes, print materials, training, etc., can be sustained if the council of the Commune's local parliament believes that reversing environmental degradation is a priority in its development plan and allocates a budget to it. Research and extension organizations, NGOs and international organizations could facilitate these processes of change.
- The Commune could facilitate the emergence of farmer organizations, which could address problems that hamper the use of knowledge, such as the absence of markets or the unavailability of fertilizers.

- The Commune should play a key role, taking the ownership of successful achievements in the field of soil fertility maintenance.

5.6 Conclusions

This case study of KM in Benin reveals that the socio-political and socio-economic changes resulting from democratization and decentralization processes have provided many opportunities. Agricultural reforms have taken place while patterns of political governance have changed. Many projects were developed to boost agricultural development. In the Commune of Ouèssè the integration of interventions by different actors enabled the development of a system of knowledge management that helped reverse land degradation and support the Mahi farmers; livelihoods. The KM activities (cultural events and folk media, rural radio programmes, training, PLAR, exchange visits, etc.) changed the Mahi farmers' perceptions about the way they were working with their environment. They still face dilemmas when it comes to making the 'right choice', that is, what knowledge should they use to reduce the degradation of their environment.

The KM strategies put in place by the Ministry of Agriculture within the National Agricultural Extension System were not effective in ensuring the continuity and sustainability of the current KM processes in the Commune of Ouèssè.

Effective KM strategies should contribute to provide an enabling institutional and policy environment for farmers, one that helps them to cope with the difficulties of maintaining soil productivity under changing conditions. This case study suggests that the Commune would be the appropriate level at which to implement a national KM strategy. At that level complex issues such as maintaining productivity given the in the specific situation of the area could be addressed, and so the livelihoods of future generations could be secured.

6 Knowledge management on natural resources in West Africa: Towards a strategy?

Suzanne Nederlof and Floris van der Pol

> *"Sharing knowledge is not about giving people something, or getting something from them. That is only valid for information sharing. Sharing knowledge occurs when people are interested in helping one another develop new capacities for action; it is about creating learning processes."*
>
> Peter Seng

Farmers spread manure on their land to keep it fertile. Pastoralists decide where to herd their animals so they can find the best grass – leaving heavily grazed areas to recover. These are examples of how people use their knowledge to manage their natural resources to produce enough to eat and to sell, as well as to conserve these resources for future use. The preceding chapters described how knowledge on natural resource management is constructed and shared. As populations grow and resources become scarcer, managing such resources sustainably is becoming ever more important.

There are different ways to learning how to manage natural resources. Scientists and development practitioners learn from farmers and other local people. The farmers can also learn from 'outsiders'. Farmers in one region learn from farmers in other regions or countries. And scientists and development practitioners gain knowledge by sharing information with each other. Are these forms of knowledge construction and sharing efficient? And if not how can they be managed to be more efficient? How can people in different areas and from different walks of life better learn from one another?

In this chapter we analyse the four preceding cases with the organisational and institutional focus introduced in Chapter 1 and conclude how to improve learning on natural resource management in a systematic way.

6.1 Knowledge management in the four cases revisited

The **Mali case study** is an example of how knowledge on soil conservation has been developed through adaptive research with cotton farmers, a process of social construction of new knowledge. Then, through an awareness raising, extension and training programme carried out by the cotton development company, the knowledge was extended to a much larger part of the rural population. We could consider this to be a combined **'industry driven'** and **'policy driven'** configuration (see Section 1.6).

The knowledge management process came to an end when, in a new policy setting, the development role of the cotton company, essentially a public-private venture, was abandoned. Since then many actors, NGOs and private consultants have appeared to work in the field of soil conservation, but none of them took the lead in sharing knowledge and jointly accumulating knowledge on new experiences. A **'joint network'** configuration did not emerge from among the competing NGOs, so much of the knowledge stayed internal in the cotton company's staff, without being shared.

A sub-regional centre for agricultural research took the initiative to create a Knowledge Platform in this multi-stakeholder setting. They started putting all internal CMDT knowledge on a CD so that it could be shared, but further knowledge sharing failed as a result of lack of interest, leadership and financial support.

The Niger case is an example an **'R&D driven'** configuration, with a (foreign) university playing a role in knowledge management. For a long time the 're-greening' of parts of the Zinder region had been overlooked by scientists. Once international scientists discovered that farmers were managing their natural resources and caring for the trees in their fields (a fact verified by aerial photographs and satellite images), they felt this knowledge should be shared with others who could make use of it. The main aim of this work was not to improve farmers' NRM, but to highlight its impact and help focus government commitment on scaling-up and re-greening other regions in Niger.

The important point in this case study is that scientists translated the impact of local farmer practices for a national and international public. Teaching programmes of both collaborating universities were adapted to incorporate the results of the study. KM activities targeting local and sub-regional actors, especially farmers, are (still) missing. Thus there is not much feedback from that group about the information provided to the targeted national and international public. Furthermore, the university led the KM process and had a vested interest in demonstrating the **newness** of what had been discovered. This 'newness' could be questioned; farmers have long maintained and cared for trees in their fields, voluntarily or enforced, eg during the reign of Sultan Tanimoum in Niger from 1854 to 1884 (Boffa/FAO 1998). This so-called 'parkland' farming system was documented a long time ago (eg Pullan 1974). For some time there have also been cycles in the green appearance of the Sahel region. If one takes as a reference point the peak of the droughts (1975) and presents these farmer practices as a new reaction to that drought, a challenging new image is indeed produced, one that well serves the knowledge manager's purpose of influencing policymakers and decision-makers. The emphasis is on **newness**, not on capitalizing on existing knowledge. This could constitute a systematic bias of research centres or universities who get credits for publishing new discoveries. Furthermore, contradictory information on increased desertification is persisting (eg Government of Niger, 2009ab) through different knowledge management configurations, presenting different discourses (de Jong, 2010).

The Togo case study presents a process of knowledge construction by social interaction, supplementing farmers' tacit knowledge, for example about their soil types and the associated soil fertility in relation to the observed healthiness of their crops, with explicit knowledge from scientists and development practitioners based on the results of fertilizer trials. Learning and action research, Farmer Field Schools and other similar activities resulted in access to new knowledge for a number of farmers through this **'development-driven'** configuration.

The project's lead NGO felt that it would be efficient to combine the activities in the different projects that they were implementing in Togo. They felt that combining different knowledge management tools would both improve their own knowledge about farmers, as well as help farmers to articulate better their knowledge needs. They engaged with government services to arrive at a national-level KM strategy, thus combining the **'development-driven'** configuration with a **'policy-driven'** configuration. However, these services appeared not to be very effective in achieving such a national strategy.

The Benin case study also presents an example of constructing knowledge through social interaction, using a configuration that is typical for much work undertaken by NGOs. Mahi farmers in the studied region had always practiced shifting cultivation and have a lot of tacit knowledge about it. Development practitioners and state actors, however, had observed major land degradation. They therefore wanted to convince the farmers to change their practices. They based their conclusion on the explicit knowledge of Mahi farming that they learned while studying how to restore the degraded soils. Thus various projects used joint learning with farmers to discover how to develop permanent intensive agriculture without degrading the resource base.

The joint learning on the basis of both types of knowledge resulted in practices that seemed acceptable to both the farmers and the developers. Yet, for Mahi farmers in less densely populated area around Ouessè, changing their practices – that is abandoning shifting cultivation and increasing investments in maintaining soil fertility under permanent cultivation – could be seriously risky.

The strength of this case study is the social construction of new knowledge that enabled the transition from shifting cultivation to more permanent agriculture. But as is often the case in sparsely populated areas, creating a more permanent agriculture appears to be difficult. The newly developed technologies apparently do not fit. Yet the knowledge managers, NGOs and state actors continue to promote this potentially flawed knowledge. Even with the national institute for agricultural research as an active partner in the project, the means or opportunities to invest in creating or identifying other technologies may be limited.

6.2   The knowledge managers and the process

These case studies present different types of knowledge managers, each having their own ways of and skills for managing knowledge according to their profile and tasks:
- **IFDC, a nonprofit international public organization**, emphasized sharing knowledge with farmers while continuing to test and develop new knowledge. This is a strong strategy; a challenge was that the intensive interaction with farmers necessary seems to limit the scale of operation. Also, with the interaction process as a focal activity, the introduction of new knowledge and research remains a challenge, as shown by the Benin case.

- **CMDT, a public-private company**, carried out a major soil conservation extension campaign. This is a typical example of the French system of engaging small producers in cash crop production, constituting a kind of public-private venture. The CMDT was large enough to have a long-term vision and implement a large soil-conservation programme.
- Later, **IER, the national public knowledge institute**, tried to keep part of the knowledge management process going, a challenge were the organizational capacity and financial resources to succeed.
- **The University of Amsterdam and Niger University** created knowledge about re-greening farmer fields and then shared it at national and international levels with policymakers, donors, scientists and students. Farmers were not included as a main target audience.

Initial phase

All these case studies concern a form of socially constructed knowledge about maintaining land's productivity, technology developed through interactions between local knowledge and formal scientific knowledge on soil fertility and conservation. The Togo case study describes the social construction of the knowledge on soil fertility management. In the case of Mali, in the first phase knowledge on feasible soil-conservation techniques was constructed through collaborations between cotton growers, the cotton company and the research institute. The Benin case study concerns a similar process. In the case of Niger, however, during the initial study phase knowledge was constructed by confronting farmers with aerial photographs and satellite images that showed the results of their behaviour in protecting trees in their fields.

If one of the partners in a knowledge construction process has less influence in the process, this could lead to a kind of 'apparent' knowledge, as could have happened in Benin, where the partners agree that soil degradation takes place. But the developed and **apparently** accepted solutions of intensive permanent cultivation are not really put into practice. Thus knowledge with respect to the problem has been shared well, but knowledge with respect to the solutions seems not to have been fully shared; the researcher might not be fully aware of all the financial consequences and risks of the proposed solutions, while the farmers might overlook the long-term benefits. Unequal financial means between partners, as in often the case in **'development-driven'** configurations, might easily lead to a distortion of the knowledge construction process.

Scaling up

After the initial knowledge construction the scaling-up process was different in each of the four cases studies. In Benin and Togo the social interaction process with the farmers was continued and supplemented with training and awareness raising to reach a larger target group. In Togo the producer organizations facilitated the knowledge-sharing process. In both cases they tried to scale up knowledge sharing to a national level with different target groups (other organizations, policymakers), but this was difficult in the actual knowledge-management configurations.

In Mali, initial knowledge construction was followed by a massive awareness-raising campaign, extension, and a 'training of trainers' approach. Knowledge sharing continued between the targeted groups of farmers and the cotton company, who managed the accumulation of knowledge at a national level (later on, in a different multi-stakeholder setting, this appeared to be difficult to continue).

In Niger, after the initial knowledge construction, the knowledge management process did not focus on the farmers, but on other target groups: policymakers, donors and scientists on the one hand, and students of the University of Niger on the other. Apparently the dispersed local knowledge management was not able to lift the knowledge on re-greening to the national and international policy levels; an external university and satellite images were needed to do this, while at the same time other configurations presented evidence for desertification.

In all the cases knowledge about natural resource management has been built up through interactions between producers, NGOs, researchers and other knowledge-service providers in different knowledge management configurations. Combining knowledge management configurations and introducing more partners into a scaling-up process appears to be difficult.

Follow up and sustainability of knowledge management

In the Niger case study, institutional sustainability seems fairly guaranteed. The University of Niger integrated the results into its education programme and decision-makers promoted the results. These better outcomes may be partly related to the target group, scientists and policymakers. Universities have well-understood roles and ways of organizing this type of knowledge management.

For the 'NGO' cases in Togo and Benin, knowledge management is part of their R&D and extension activities. As long as the NGOs continue to be funded, there is no direct need to make special provisions for institutional sustainability of their type of knowledge management; many NGOs focus their activities on extension and training, both knowledge management activities. But if the NGOs cease their activities, institutional and financial sustainability are not ensured.

The Mali case study is an example of how, after an initial sustainable-looking institutional approach, changes in the macro-economic context caused problems with respect to the sustainability of knowledge management. It might be efficient to have the role of knowledge manager performed by one big organization, but such organizations do not last forever. The solution proposed was to use a knowledge management platform organized by cotton region's knowledge institute (IER). There was insufficient support from the government and donors, however, partly because it was not clear how the activity could be financed in the long run. This weakness is at the same time a challenge. Formerly, the public-private cotton venture led the knowledge management process, thus limiting the role of the producers in organizing their knowledge. Now the producers have to organize knowledge management themselves, or ensure its organisation. For instance they could – or their organizations could – stimulate development of a high-quality training programme that service providers in training and extension should follow to get certified. However producer's ability to manage knowledge – especially of topics with long time horizon, such as natural resource management – has still to be proved.

6.3 Coming to a knowledge management strategy

The examples of 'knowledge management' presented in these four case studies show what practitioners have done in the area of natural resource management. As is evident from the descriptions, no clear knowledge management strategy had been designed at the start of any of the projects. In practice, strategies and approaches were developed during the actual work, fitting the genuine insights and needs of the 'knowledge manager'. Thus the objective of the activity clearly determines what kind of knowledge management is carried out and which approach is used. This helped to keep thinking about knowledge management pragmatic.

The case studies clearly show that knowledge service providers develop their own approach to knowledge management, depending on their specific tasks, skills and insights, confirming the configurations identified earlier. Knowledge management strategies will have to take into account these preferences and the skills of the many actors.

The strength of most local knowledge service providers (especially NGOs) is that they work closely with farmers. However, it seems their work is difficult to scale up. This would require more structure in the knowledge service providers themselves to enable them to efficiently share knowledge and learn from each other. But even if the will is there, the demand side that should push for better knowledge sharing is weakly organized. The low organizational capacity of the farmers, together with their limited experience in formal learning, hampers the scaling up of knowledge management activities by NGOs.

In West Africa, strong organizations working with large groups of farmers are scarce, thus one continues to work with the existing small and fragmented knowledge services that barely share knowledge with each other and are not really able to make an impact at national policy and donor levels.

Scaling up knowledge management with policymakers and scientists seems to be easier, possibly because within those groups written information is more easily transformed into knowledge (as these groups are more practised at learning from written information). However, since the farmers are not included, the process is easily distorted. Conflicting information is presented about natural resources use. For important issues like desertification or land grabbing, farmers' feedback in the knowledge management system at national policy level is essential.

This situation is presented in Figure 10. In Benin and Togo, KM was tried at higher levels. In Mali this had to be abandoned (see the stripes on Figure 10). In Niger high-level of knowledge sharing with policymakers was achieved, but not supported by high-level knowledge sharing with farmers. In the field of natural resource management, high-level knowledge sharing with farmers is still lacking, as indicated by the void in the upper right-hand corner of Figure 10. This has two important consequences:

- Most of the locally constructed knowledge stays local and is not used widely by other farmers.
- Knowledge exchange between farmers and policymakers is too limited, leading to contradictory policies and donor interventions and slow reactions to new situations.

Figure 10 Institutional setting for scaling up knowledge management in the four case studies

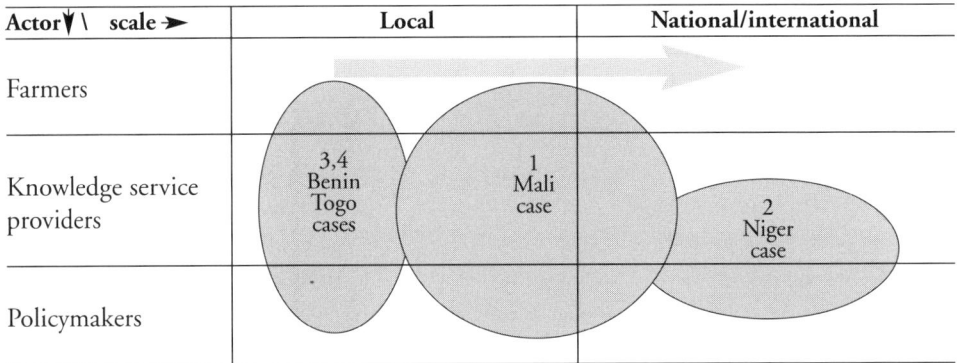

It is our feeling that any strategy for knowledge management of natural resources would require the construction of a knowledge management configuration that was able to fill that void. In the present conditions, however, there is no reason to be optimistic about achieving this, especially because in the field of natural resource management the relationship between actions and consequences are slow.

As a result, knowledge is built up slowly, and thus knowledge management is less interesting for many small knowledge service providers with a short time horizon. Knowledge management at national and international levels that engaged farmers in the process would require the combined operation of different knowledge management configurations. This proved to be difficult to realize.

We see four strategic issues that need to be addressed to improve knowledge management on the sustainable use of natural resources in Western Africa:
- First, the rural producers' influence on the KM process is still very limited. This can easily create **apparent** knowledge, as we saw in Benin. Furthermore, their absence is the main cause of the weak institutional (and thus financial) sustainability of knowledge management. Rural producers' influence on the process should be strengthened by increasing both their technical and organizational capacities. Adult education and rural development programmes are important tools to achieve this.
- Second, much remains to be learned about KM in a multi-stakeholder environment at the national level. At the local levels NGOs play an important role. At the higher regional, national, or even macro-regional levels, platforms could be created to share knowledge between different NGOs, representatives of producer organizations and scientists. Yet, the main question remains – who would take the lead in such a process?

- Third, the sustainable use of natural resources in rural development is frequently considered to be an environmental issue, and as such falls within the mandate of the environmental ministries, who traditionally focus more on issues such as forestry, biodiversity and wildlife. Ministries of Agriculture in West Africa need to take more responsibility for stimulating the long-term productivity of natural resources in rural areas. With renewed attention for agricultural development there might be a new chance for this.
- Finally, with the many donor organizations each following their own preferences, it is unlikely that knowledge management will be a policy priority for them. Are their time horizons sufficiently long? Would they accept a leader in the process? We advocate that donors make available a percentage of their contributions to rural development programmes to establish joint knowledge management systems for sustainable natural resource use.

In today's development scene, much is expected from strengthening the technical and organizational capacities of producers and their organizations, who could then take the lead in forcing the present fragmented multi-stakeholder landscape of knowledge services to learn better from each other's experiences and to put consistent information on the desks of policymakers and donors. In the meantime configurations and potential leaders need to be identified that could successfully take up KM activities at the national level.

References

Chapter 1

Barbiero, Daniel (n.d.) Tacit knowledge, in: Chris Eliasmith, ed. *Dictionary of philosophy of mind*. St. Louis, MO: Washington University in St. Louis. http://www.artsci.wustl.edu/~philos/MindDict/tacitknowledge.html.

Barnard, G., S. Smits, K. Santi and B. Collins (2006) 'What's happening with KM in multilateral and bilateral development agencies?' Discussions at the KM4Dev Annual Meeting, July 2006. http://www.km4dev.org/wiki/index.php/What%E2%80%99s_Happening_with_KM_in_Multilateral_and_Bilateral_Development_Agencies%3F

Batjes, N.H. (1995a) 'A global data set of soil pHproperties', *Tech. Pap.* 27, ISRIC, Wageningen.

Batjes, N.H. (1995b) 'World Inventory of Soil Emission Potentials: WISE 2.1 – Database user's manual and coding protocols', *Tech. Pap.* 26, ISRIC, Wageningen.

Bhowmik, A. (2006) 'Framework for solving global problems: a case study using TRIZ', *Triz Journal* 8(7), 5 pp. http://www.triz-journal.com/archives/2006/08/07.pdf#search=%22Framework%20for%20solving%20global%20problems%3A%20a%20case%20study%20using%20TRIZ%22

Buchholz, G. (2005) Information and Knowledge Management (IKM) Systems within the context of Natural Resource Management in Southeast Asia Experiences from 25 Years of German Technical Cooperation. http://www2.gtz.de/dokumente/bib/05-0440.pdf#search=%22IKM%20GTZ%20Buchholz%22

Clark, L. (2006) 'Building farmers' capacities for networking (Part II): Strengthening agricultural supply chains in Bolivia using network analysis', *Knowledge Management for Development Journal* 2(2), 19-32. http://www.km4dev.org/journal/index.php/km4dj/article/view/64/106

Davies, J. (2006) Symposium 2: Mobilizing Science and Communities to Combat Land Degradation: Role of Knowledge Management and Indicators for Optimizing Impact. FORUM on 'Sustainable Land and Water Management: A GEF Agenda for Combating Environmental Degradation and Promoting Sustainable Livelihoods. The third GEF assembly 2006. http://www.gefweb.org/3rd_assembly/Background_Note_Symposium_2.pdf#search=%22Knowledge%20Management%20for%20SLM%20Davies%22

Dixon, J. and A. Gulliver (2001) *Farming Systems and Poverty, improving farmers' livelihoods in a changing world*, D. Gibbon (Principal Editor): FAO/Malcolm Hall. http://www.fao.org/DOCREP/003/Y1860E/Y1860E00.HTM

Douthwaite, B., A. Carvajal, S. Alvarez, E. Claros and L.A. Hernández (2006) 'Building farmers' capacities for networking (Part I): Strengthening rural groups in Colombia through network analysis', *Knowledge Management for Development Journal* 2(2), 4-18. http://www.km4dev.org/journal/index.php/km4dj/article/view/63/116

Douthwaite, B. (2006/7). *Enabling Innovation, Technology- and System-Level Approaches that Capitalize on Complexity*. Mitpress.mit.edu/innovations (2006). http://boru.pbworks.com/f/INNOV0104_douthwaite.pdf

Egulu, B. and P. Ebanyat (2000). Policy Processes in Uganda and their Impact on Soil Fertility.

Managing Africa's Soils No 16, IIED, London.

Elias, M., J. Bayala and M. Dianda (2006) 'Impediments and innovations in knowledge sharing: the case of the African shea sector', *Knowledge Management for Development Journal* 2(1): 52-67. http://www.km4dev.org/journal/index.php/km4dj/article/view/52/95#search=%22cotton%20knowledge%20management%20Africa%22

Engel, P. and Salomon, M. (1997) *Facilitating innovation for development: a RAAKS resource box.* Amsterdam, Royal Tropical Institute.

FAO (1998) *World reference base for soil resources.* FAO, Rome, 1998. M-41 (ISBN 92-5-104141-5). http://www.fao.org/docrep/W8594E/W8594E00.htm

FAO (2006) Knowledge management profile. Unpublished resource, KM4Dev website. http://www.km4dev.org/index.php/articles/727

FAO (2004) 'Scaling soil nutrient balances. Enabling mesolevel applications for African realities', *FAO Fertilizer and Plant Nutrition Bulletin* 15, FAO, Rome.

FAO/KIT (2005) *Integrating environmental and economic accounting at the farm level. Accounting for changes in the fertility of cultivated land.* FAO Rome, 2005 Agricultural Support Systems Division, FAO Agriculture Department KIT – Royal Tropical Institute, The Netherlands. http://www.fao.org/ag/ags/subjects/en/farmmgmt/pdf/environmental/main_book.pdf

Franzluebbers, K., L.R. Hossner, and A.S.R. Jou (1998) 'Integrated nutrient management for sustained crop production in Sub-Saharan Africa (a review)'. Soil Management (CRSP), *TropSoils Bulletin* 98-03, Texas A&M University, USA.

Heijden, A. van der, T. Pryor and Lars T. Soeftestad (2006) 'Knowledge management and natural resources in Africa: perspectives from two networks', *Knowledge Management for Development Journal* 2(1): 105-118. http://www.km4dev.org/journal/index.php/km4dj/article/view/57/99#search=%22knowledge%20management%20and%20natural%20resource%20management%22

Henderson, K. (2005) 'The knowledge sharing approach of the United Nations Development Programme', *Knowledge Management for Development Journal* 1(2): 19-30. http://www.km4dev.org/journal/index.php/km4dj/article/view/21/17

Hilhorst, T. and G. Baltissen (eds) (2004) *La décentralisation au Mali: du discours a la pratique.* Bulletin No. 358. Amsterdam: Royal Tropical Institute. http://www.kit.nl/net/KIT_Publicaties_output/ShowFile2.aspx?e=593

ICARDA (2006) Megaproject 6: Knowledge management and dissemination for sustainable development in Dry Areas. In: ICARDA Medium Term Plan 2006-2008. Unpublished paper, 9 pp. http://www.icarda.org/MTP/2006-2008/Megaproject6.pdf#search=%22IFAD%20%22knowledge%20management%22%22

Lightfoot, C. and U. Scheuermeier (2006) Linking Local Learners: building knowledge management strategies for effective rural development in East Africa. Progress Report. Activities from January to April 2006. Unpublished report, 19 pp. http://www.linkinglearners.net/downloads/ProgressReport.pdf#search=%22IFAD%20%22knowledge%20management%22%22

Liniger, H.P, G.W.J. van Lynden and G. Schwilch (2002) Documenting field knowledge for better land management decisions – experiences with WOCAT tools in local, national and global programs. Proceedings of ISCO Conference 2002, Vol. I, pp. 259-167. Beijing. http://www.wocat.net/MATERIALS/ISCOdocu.pdf#search=%22ISRIC%20knowledge%20management%22

Matovelo, D.S, J. Msuya and Egbert de Smet (2005?) Towards developing proactive information acquisition practices among smallholder farmers for empowerment and poverty reduction: a situation analysis. Unpublished paper, 12 pp. http://www.livelihoods.org/post/Docs/IAALD/021Matovelo.doc

Mchombu K. (2003) 'Information dissemination for development: an impact study', *Information Development* 19(2):111-125.

Ministère de l'Agriculture, Burkina Faso (1999) Stratégie nationale et plan d'action de gestion intégrée de la fertilité des sols (PAGIFS).

Ministère de l'Agriculture, de l'Hydraulique et des ressources halieutiques, Burkina Faso (2003) Plan d'Action pour la Gestion Intégrée des Ressources en Eau du Burkina Faso (PAGIRE).

Pels, J. and F. Odhiambo (2005) 'Design of and practical experiences with the Learn@WELL knowledge management module', *Knowledge Management for Development Journal*, 1 (2), p. 4-18. http://www.km4dev.org/journal/index.php/km4dj/article/viewFile/20/59

Pineiro, M. (2005) Strengthening research for developing capacities: national, regional and global science capacity. CGIAR, Unpublished note, 8 pp. http://www.cgiar.org/meetings/agm05/stakeholders_docs/agm05_stake_5b_pineiro.pdf#search=%22Strengthening%20research%20for%20developing%20capacities%3A%20national%2C%20regional%20and%20global%20science%20capacity.%20%22

Pol, F. van der (1992) *Soil mining: An unseen contributor to farm income in southern Mali*. Bulletin no. 325. Amsterdam: Royal Tropical Institute.

Polanyi, M. (1958). Personal knowledge: towards a post-critical philosophy. Chicago, IL: University of Chicago Press. Cited in Wilson (2002).

Quaggiotto, G. (2005) 'Elective affinities? Reflections on the enduring appeal of knowledge management for the development sector', *Knowledge Management for Development Journal* 1(3): 41-45. http://www.km4dev.org/journal/index.php/km4dj/article/view/37

Ramalingam, B. (2006) *Tools for knowledge and learning: a guide for development and humanitarian organisations*. Working Paper No. 244, London: Overseas Development Institute, 94 pp. http://www.odi.org.uk/Rapid/Publications/Documents/KM_toolkit_web.pdf

Visscher, J.T, J. Pels, V. Markowski and Sascha de Graaf (2006) *Knowledge and information management in the water and sanitation sector: a hard nut to crack*. Thematic Overview paper No.14, 66 pp. http://www.irc.nl/content/download/25395/280851/file/TOP14_KM_06.pdf

Wilson, T.D. (2002) *The nonsense of 'knowledge management'*. Information Research, Vol. 8 No. 1, October 2002. http://www.informationr.net/ir/8-1/paper144.html

World Bank (1998) *Knowledge for Development*, World Development Report No.21, World Bank, Washington, DC. http://www.worldbank.org/wdr/wdr98/index.htm

Chapter 2

Bishop J. and J. Allen (1989) *The on-site cost of soil erosion in Mali*. Environmental Department, World Bank, Working Paper 21, Washington.

Bodnár F. and J. de Graaff (2003) 'Factors influencing adoption of soil and water conservation in southern Mali' *Land Degradation and Development* 14: 515-25.

Bodnár, F., T. Schrader and W. Van Campen (2006) 'How project approach influences adoption of SWC by farmers, examples from southern Mali', *Land Degradation & Development* 17, 5 (2006), p. 453-570.

Bosma R., K. Bengaly, M. Traoré and A. Roeleveld (1996) *L'élevage en voie d'intensification. Synthèse de la recherche sur les ruminants dans les exploitations agricoles mixtes au Mali-Sud*. Edition KIT, Systèmes de production rurale au Mali 3, Amsterdam/Bamako.

Campen, W. van (1991) 'The long road to sound land management in southern Mali', In: A. Huisman (eds), *Making haste slowly: strengthening local environmental management in agricultural development*, pp. 131-48. Royal Tropical Institute, Amsterdam.

CMDT (1995) *Programmes détaillés. Proposition d'un programme d'apui des bailleurs de fonds auprès de la CMDT* (1996-2000). Actions vocation centrale. CMDT, Bamako.

CMDT (1996) *Maintien du potentiel productif et développement rural en zone CMDT*. DDRS, CMDT, Koutiala.

Hallam, G.M. and W. van Campen (1985) Reacting to farmers complaints of soil erosion on agriculturally intensive farms in southern Mali: from fixed answers to flexible reponse. Presented at Soil Conservation and Productivity, Maracay, Venezuela. Sociedad Venezolano de la Sciencia del Suelo.

Hallam, G.M. and K. Verbeek (1986) *Travaux anti-érosives faits par les paysans en zone Mali-Sud*. Une évaluation économique. IER / KIT, Bamako / Amsterdam.

Hijkoop, J, P. van der Poel and B. Kaya (1991) *Une lutte de longue haleine*. IER / KIT, Systèmes de production rurale au Mali Sikasso/Amsterdam.

Jansen, L. and S. Diarra (1992) *Mali-Sud, étude diachronique des surfaces agricoles*. KIT, Amsterdam.

Joldersma, R., T. Hilhorst, S. Diarra, L. Coulibaly and J.C.J. Vlaar (1994) *Siwaa, la brousse sèche. Expérience de gestion de terroir villageois au Mali*. Bulletin no. 341. Amsterdam: Royal Tropical Institute.

MaliArp (1999) *Cartographie des infrastructures communales*. Fox Media, Meylan.

Mourik, D. van, M. Niang and A. Mohammedoune (1993) *Système de suivi évluation CMDT pour la LAE et GRN. Préparé dans le cadre d'une mission d'appui à la CMDT pour le PLAE*. DDRS, CMDT, Bamako.

PLAE (1986) *Plan d'opération du PLAE dans la zone Mali-Sud, 1986-1989*. CMDT-IRRT, Sikasso.

PLAE (1989) *Plan d'opération du PLAE dans la zone Mali-Sud, deuxième phase 1989-1993*. DG, CMDT, Bamako.

Pol, F. van der (1992) *Soil mining: an unseen contributor to farm income in southern Mali*. Bulletin. Amsterdam: Royal Tropical Institute.

Roose, E. (1985) *Rapport de mission aupres de la DRSPR dans la région Mali-Sud*. Montpellier.

Schrader, T. (1997) *Le système de suivi de la CMDT et les indicateurs de performance des programmes appuyés par la Coopération néerlandaise*. DTDR, CMDT, Bamako.

Schrader T.H. and B.H. Wennink (1996) *La lutte anti érosive en zone CMDT*. Rapport final du PLAE. CMDT / KIT, Bamako / Amsterdam.

Schrader T.H., B.H. Wennink, W.J. Veldkamp and T. Defoer (eds) (1998) 'Natural resource management in the cotton zone of southern Mali: merging farmer participatory research, extension and policy', *Closing the loop: from research on natural resources to policy change*, pp. 142-55. SCDPM, Maastricht.

Vlot, J.E. and M. Traoré (1994) *Etude des toposéquences cercle de Koutiala*. Rapport d'étape: campagne 1993. IER, Sikasso.

Chapter 3

Baoua, I. (2006). *Analyse des impacts des investissements dans la gestion des ressources naturelles sur le secteur élevage dans les régions de Maradi, Tahoua et Tillabéry au Niger*. Centre Régional d'Enseignement Spécialisé en Agriculture (CRESA), Niamey, Etude Sahélienne. See also http://www.cilss.bf/IMG/pdf/etudesahelrapportNE.pdf

Irz, X, Lin Lin , C. Thirtle and S. Wiggins (2002) Agricultural Productivity Growth and Poverty Alleviation. *Development Policy Review Volume* 19 Issue 4, Pages 449-466.

Larwanou, M. et Saadou (2006). Evaluation de la flore et de la végétation dans les sites traités et non dans les régions de Tahoua, Maradi et Tillabéry. Centre Régional d'Enseignement Spécialisé en Agriculture (CRESA), Niamey, Etude Sahélienne. Cited in http://www.cilss.bf/IMG/pdf/etudesahelrapportNE.pdf

Larwanou, M., M. Abdoulaye and C. Reij (2006) *Etude de la régénération naturelle assistée dans la Région de Zinder (Niger): une première exploration d'un phénomène spectaculaire*. Washington, International Resources Group/USAID.

Mortimore, M. , M.Tiffen, B.Yamba et J.Nelson (2001). Synthèse sur l'évolution à long terme dans le département de Maradi (Niger) 1960-2000. Also as 'Department of Maradi: Synthesis', Drylands Research Working Paper 39e. Drylands Research, Crewkerne, United Kingdom. Refers to Tiffen, M., Mortimore, M. and Gichuki, F. (1994) More people, less erosion : Environmental recovery in Machakos, Kenya. John Wiley, Chichester. http://padniger.net/Documents%20and%20Reports/Biblio/WP39f.pdf

Reij, C. (2008) *Building on a current green revolution in the Sahel*. Note prepared for the Sahel Re-greening Initiative. Center for International Cooperation VU University Amsterdam.

Rinaudo, T. (2005) *Uncovering the underground forest: a short history and description of farmer-managed natural regeneration.* Melbourne, World Vision Australia.

Tappan, G. (2009) FRAME web site post on Managed Natural Regeneration in Niger dd 2-1-2009. http://www.frameweb.org/CommunityBrowser.aspx?id=2811.

World Resources Institute (2008) 'Turning back the desert: how farmers have transformed Niger's landscapes and livelihoods', In: *Roots of resilience: growing the wealth of the poor.* pp. 142-57.

Chapter 4

Akollor, D.S. (2008) Analyse de la disparité des genres et diffusion à grande échelle des innovations GIFS au Sud Togo. Cas de Djakakopé et ses environs. Mémoire de Maîtrise en Sociologie de Développement, Université de Lomé, Togo.

Ankou, K.A. and A.F. Tamelokpo (2003) *Diagnostic Participatif de la Fertilité des Sols pour Développement et la diffusion des options GIFS. Cas des sols ferralitiques dégradés de Savane Côtière Togolaise.* IFDC-Africa, Lomé, Togo.

Brabant, P., S. Darracq, K. Egué, and V. Simonneaux (1996) Togo: 'Etat de dégradation des terres résultant des activités humaines', *Collection notice explicative* No.112. Paris: Editions de l'ORSTOM.

Deffo, V., S. Hounzangbé-Adoté, R. Maliki, and M.E. Ould Ferroukh (1999) 'Options d'intensification durable des cultures vivrières au Sud Togo'. Etude ICRA & IFDC-Afrique. Document de Travail No. 33, Montpellier, France.

Engel, P.H. and M.L. Salomon (1997) *Facilitating innovation for development.* A RAAKS Resource box. KIT: Amsterdam.

FAO (1995) Togo. Préparation d'un plan de restructuration des institutions rurales. Rapport de synthèse de la deuxième étape du projet: Propositions de restructuration et plan de mise en œuvre. Projet TCP/TOG 4451. Lomé (Togo): FAO.

Gross, M. and G. Ezui (eds) (2005) *Boîte à outils AISSA: Faciliter l'intensification agricole, une centaine d'outils pour développer les marchés et les technologies au niveaux local.* Lomé (Togo): AISSA Network and IFDC-Africa.

IFDC and TSBF-CIAT (2005) 'Development and dissemination of sustainable integrated soil fertility management practices for smallholder farms in Sub-Saharan Africa', *Technical Bulletin* IFDC T-7. 1Muscle Shoals: IFDC

ISNAR (1995) 'Composante recherche du projet de restructuration des institutions rurales. Volume 1: Diagnostic de la recherche agricole'. ISNAR country report No.R58. La Haye: Service International pour la Recherche Agricole Nationale 9ISNAR).

Lamboni, D., K.A. Ankou, and A.F. Tamelokpo (2003) Curriculum DATE-R pour la Gestion Intégrée de la Fertilité des Sols.

Maatman, A., C. Dangbégnon, and H. Van Reuler (2001) IFDC-'Africa's experiences in the development of integrated soil fertility management strategies at the village and regional level in West Africa', In: R.N. Roy and H. Nabhan (eds), *Soil and Nutrient Management in Sub-Saharan Africa in support of the Soil Fertility Initiative*, pp. 297-308. Proceedings of the Expert Consultation, Lusaka, Zambia, 6-9 December 1999. Rome: FAO.

Maatman, A., B. Kézié, C. Dangbégnon, and M. Schreurs (2000) *Integrated soil fertility management: a key for rural development.* Lomé (Togo): IFDC-Africa.

Meertens, B. (2001) *La riziculture irriguée dans la vallée de Zio. Région Maritime du Togo. Contraintes et possibilités.* IFDC-Division Afrique, Lomé, Togo.

Reuler, H. van, and A.F. Tamelokpo (1998) 'A farmer-oriented approach to soil fertility managment including the creation of a revolving fund – a case study from the southern Togo', In: P. Drechsel and Gyiele (eds) *On-farm research on sustainable land management in Sub-Saharan Africa: Approaches, Experiences, and lessons.* Proceedings based on paers from international meeting held at Abengourou, Côte d'Ivoire, 11-22 August 1997, (pp. 65-72).

World Bank (2003) *Togo: Stratégie de croissance du secteur agricole et rural.* Banque Mondiale, Lomé, Togo.

Chapter 5

Amadji, F., I. Adjé, R. Maliki,, and K. Téblékou (2007) 'Promotion des systèmes de semis direct sous couverture végétale au Bénin: état des lieux, travaux de terrain et perspectives'. Papier présenté à Maroua (Cameroun). INRAB, Cotonou, Bénin.

Amadji, F., S. Tarawali and K. Ahouanton (2004a) *Le Mucuna: pour une amélioration durable de la fertilité du sol et des rendements des cultures au Centre et au sud du Bénin.* BMZ-GTZ/ILRI-IITA, INRAB-PULH/ AFD-PADSE, Cotonou, Bénin.

Amadji, F., S. Tarawali and K. Ahouanton (2004b) *Aeschynomenea: pour une amélioration durable de la fertilité du sol et des rendements des cultures au Centre et au sud du Bénin.* BMZ-GTZ/ILRI-IITA, INRAB-PULH/AFD-PADSE, Cotonou, Bénin.

Amadji, F., S. Tarawali and K. Ahouanton (2005) *Stylosanthes: pour une amélioration durable de la fertilité du sol et des rendements des cultures au Centre et au sud du Bénin.* BMZ-GTZ/ILRI-IITA, INRAB-PULH/ AFD-PADSE, Cotonou, Bénin.

Anignikin, Sylvain C. (2001) 'Histoire des populations mahi. À propos de la controverse sur l'ethnonyme et le toponyme «Mahi»*', *Cahiers d'études africaines*, 162, http://etudesafricaines.revues.org/document86.html

Ankou, K.A. and A.F. Tamelokpo (2003) *Diagnostic Participatif de la Fertilité des Sols pour Développement et la diffusion des options GIFS. Cas des sols ferralitiques dégradés de Savane Côtière Togolaise.* IFDC-Africa, Lomé, Togo.

Dangbégnon, C. (1998) 'Rural Developments in the Western part of the Sous-Préfecture of OUESSE, Benin', In: L. Hoefsloot (ed.) *Land use planning and negotiating platforms.* Wageningen: DLO Winand Staring Centre for Integrated Land, Soil and Water Research (SC-DLO).

Dangbégnon, C. (1994) 'Différentes approches de la Vulgarisation Agricole au Bénin', In: P. Linde & I. Riemersa (eds) *Arrière-plan: réflexions sur l'innovation Agricole.* Peter Linde Production, Wageningen, Les Pays-Bas.

Dangbégnon, C. (1999) 'Managing watersheds in Benin' (pp. 26-7). In: M.C. Monroe, *What works? A guide to environmental education and communication projects for practitioners and donors.* Washington DC: Academy for Educational Development & Gabriola Island: New Society Publishers.

Dangbégnon, C., A. Blum., E.S. Nederlof, N. Röling and R. Tossou (2001) *Platform for Sustainable Natural Resource Management: The West Africa case.* KIT, Amsterdam.

Djohossou, P. (1993) *Approche et stratégies d'intervention du volet Aménagement des Bassins Versants du PGRN.* MDR/DFRN/PGRN, Cotonou, Bénin.

Engel, P.H. and M.L. Salomon (1997) *Facilitating innovation for development. A RAAKS Resource Box.* KIT: Amsterdam.

FAO (2000) *Guidelines and reference material on integrated soil and nutrient management and conservation for Farmer Field Schools.* Rome: FAO.

Lamboni, D., K.A. Ankou, and A.F. Tamelokpo (2003) *Curriculum DATE-R pour la Gestion Intégrée de la Fertilité des Sols.*

Maatman, A., C. Dangbégnon and H. Van Reuler (2001) 'FDC-Africa's experiences in the development of integrated soil fertility management strategies at the village and regional level in West Africa', In: R.N. Roy and H. Nabhan (eds), *Soil and Nutrient Management in Sub-Saharan Africa in support of the Soil Fertility Initiative*, pp. 297-308. Proceedings of the Expert Consultation, Lusaka, Zambia, 6-9 December 1999. Rome: FAO.

Maatman, A., B. Kézié, C. Dangbégnon, and M. Schreurs (2000) *Integrated soil fertility management: a key for rural development.* Lomé (Togo): IFDC-Africa.

Ouikoun, M. Maurice, M. Imorou-Karimou and A. Tokou-Dada (2005) *Etude sur l'analyse des services – Conseils Agricoles au Bénin.* Rapport de Consultation. MAEP & Banque Mondiale, Cotonou Bénin.

World Bank (2003) *Project performance Assessment Report: Agricultural Services Restructuring Project (Credit 22850, TF 21619)*, Report No.26 26207, World Bank, Cotonou (Benin).

World Bank (2008) *Africa Development indicators.*

Chapter 6

Boffa, J.-M, FAO CONSERVATION GUIDE 34. *Agroforestry parklands in sub-Saharan Africa.* FAO 1998. http://www.fao.org/docrep/005/X3940E/X3940E00.HTM

Government of Niger (2009a). Conseil des Ministres du 20 janvier 2009 sur la gestion du bassin versant de Badaguichiri. http://www.presidence.ne/article.php?id_article=269.

Government of Niger, 2009b. Contribution du Niger A la Réunion de Consultation pour la Plate forme Régionale Africaine en Réduction des Risques de Catastrophe. http://74.125.77.132/search?q=cache:7eiRrpfjVwJ:www.acmad.org/en/bibliotheque/ISDR

Jong, A.A. de, (2010) Verwoestijning of vergroening. Wat gebeurt er in de Sahel? *Geografie* Nr 2.

Pullan, R.A. 1974. Farmed parkland in West Africa. *Savanna* 3(2): 119-151.

About the authors

Mathias Dotou Ahounou is an agronomist and has a long experience in capacity building in the agricultural sector and in the promotion and dissemination of agricultural innovations. He is an expert of multi-actor facilitation processes. With a background in institutional development of professional and non-governmental organizations, he has over 19 years of work experiences with international, national and grassroots' organizations. He joined IFDC in 2007 and is currently the coordinator and agribusiness cluster advisor in Benin for the 1000s+ project. mahounou@ifdc.org

Ferko Bodnár is a tropical crop scientist, with a focus on production ecology and resource conservation. He lived and worked over 8 years in Africa, first for the Malawi Agroforestry Extension Project, later for the Malian Cotton and Rural Development Programme. He holds a PhD based on the evaluation of the long-term soil and water conservation programme in South Mali. Since 2004 he is employed as advisor tropical agriculture at Agro Eco – Louis Bolk Institute, focusing on sustainable and organic agriculture, value chain development, and project design and evaluation. f.bodnar@agrevalue.nl

Sarah Cummings has 25 years' experience in the area of information and knowledge for development. She is currently Senior Consultant, Knowledge Management at Context, international cooperation in The Netherlands. She is Editor-in-Chief of the Knowledge Management for Development Journal, member of the management team of the Information and Knowledge Management Emergent Research Programme www.ikmemergent.net, and member of the Advisory Board of Hivos. Sarah blogs, with colleagues at: thegiraffe.wordpress.com

Constant Dangbegnon holds a PhD in social sciences and has over 19 years of experience in numerous West African countries in various fields that are relevant for improving Sustainable Livelihoods of farmers. He joined IFDC – Africa Division in June 1999 as a socio-economist and extension specialist. Since 2006, he joined the Natural Research Management Program as a social scientist/agronomist for the Sub-Sahara Africa Challenge Program and his activities focus on the development of innovation platforms to improve smallholder farmers livelihoods in the Kano – Katsina – Maradi pilot learning site in the Northern Region of Nigeria.
cdangbegnon@ifdc.org

Gustave Azankpo Kpagbin is an associate researcher in soil science and expert in integrated soil fertility management. He has over 28 years of experiences in soil resources management in the Beninese agricultural research & development system. He is currently the head of Soil Fertility Division of the *Laboratoire des Sciences du Sol, Eaux et Environnement,* a laboratory of the national agricultural research institute of Benin (INRAB). Mr. Kpagbin is a facilitator of community processes to link farmer groups to agricultural input dealers to promote adoption and adaptation of soil fertility management options by smallholders.
gkpagbin@yahoo.fr

Mahamane Larwanou is a forestry ecologist and a member of the national research team undertaking the Sahel study in Niger. He is currently attached to the African Forest Forum based in Nairobi.
m.larwanou@cgiar.org

Abdoulaye Mando is a soil management specialist with over 19 years research and outreach experience. He is currently the NRMP leader for the IFDC-Division for Africa and in this capacity has provided leadership and strategic guidance to numerous projects on integrated soil fertility management, fertilizer accessibility and innovation systems, working with various donors.
amando@ifdc.org

Suzanne Nederlof is rural development sociologist with experience in platform building, experiential learning, innovation systems, farmer-based organizations and agricultural research and extension. She has more than twelve years of working experience in Sub Saharan Africa. She holds a PhD in Communication and Innovation Studies. She is presently employed as a senior advisor in sustainable economic development at the KIT Department of Development Policy and Practice in Amsterdam.
s.nederlof@kit.nl

Floris van der Pol is a specialist in management and organization of adaptive and demand-driven agricultural research and development. Presently he is engaged in chain innovation programs in Mali, linking formal research with private sector partners to improve technology for processing of agricultural products and access to markets for small producers. Furthermore he worked on technical and socio-economic aspects of soil degradation, the calculation of nutrient balances, the economics of nutrient depletion as well as on erosion control and related policies.
f.v.d.pol@kit.nl

Chris Reij is a human geographer, who has worked in the Sahel since 1978. He is a senior natural resource management specialist of the Centre for International Cooperation, VU University Amsterdam. At the time of writing he was coordinator of a Sahel study, which analyzed long-term trends in agriculture and environment in four Sahel countries. At present he is facilitator of African Re-greening Initiatives.
CP.Reij@cis.vu.nl

Zana Jean-Luc Sanogo is agronomist and presently head of the research programme on agricultural mechanization of the Centre for Experimentation and Education on Mechanization in Agriculture in Mali. From 1980 to 2007 he worked as researcher at the *Institut d'Economie Rurale* in the team on farming systems and natural resource management, becoming team leader in 1998. In that position he contributed to development of methods for participatory research institutionalizing communication and knowledge exchange between farmers, researchers and developers especially in the field of natural resource management.
zjlsanogo@yahoo.fr

Adonko (Francis) Tamelokpo MSc, joined IFDC in September 1998 as agronomist. His main focus is on development of options for integrated soil fertility management. In this area he is a facilitator of participatory learning and action research which involves many actors like researchers, extension workers and farmers. He has worked for 16 years in the national agricultural research system in Togo before joining IFDC.
atamelokpo@ifdc.org

Adam Toudou is an agronomist, who has for many years been director of the *Centre Régional Spécialisé en Agriculture* of the University of Niamey. He has coordinated the Sahel study in Niger, which identified and analyzed long-term trends in agriculture and environment.
atoudou@refer.ne

Boubacar Yamba is a biogeographer, who became a leading expert in Niger in land tenure and local institutions. He works at the University of Niamey, has extensive experience with research in the Maradi region of Niger and has been involved in numerous studies and consultancies.
byamba@refer.ne

Colophon

Bulletins of the Royal Tropical Institute (KIT)
The KIT Bulletin Series deals with current themes in international development. It is a multi-disciplinary forum to present the work of scientists, policy makers, managers and development advisors in agriculture, natural resource management, health, culture, history and anthropology. These fields reflect the broad scope of KIT's activities.

KIT Development Policy & Practice
KIT Development Policy & Practice is the Royal Tropical Institute's main department for international development. Our aim is to contribute to reducing poverty and inequality in the world and to support sustainable development. We carry out research and provide advisory services and training in order to build and share knowledge on a wide range of development issues. We work in partnership with higher education, knowledge and research institutes, non-governmental and civil society organizations, and responsible private enterprises in countries around the world.

Contact information
Royal Tropical Institute (KIT)
KIT Development Policy & Practice
PO Box 95001
1090 HA Amsterdam
The Netherlands
Telephone: +31 (0)20 568 8458
Fax: +31 (0)20 568 8444
Email: development@kit.nl
Website: www.kit.nl/development

© 2010 KIT, Amsterdam, The Netherlands

This is an open access publication distributed under the terms of the Creative Commons Attribution Licence which permits unrestricted use, distribution and reproduction in any medium, provided the original author and source are credited.

This work was supported by a contribution from the Netherlands Ministry of Foreign Affairs. The content of this publication is the responsibility of the authors and does not necessarily reflect the views of the Ministry.

Edited by Kimberly Clarke
Cover and design Studio Berry Slok, Amsterdam, the Netherlands
Cover photo Roel Burgler
Printing High Trade BV, Zwolle, the Netherlands

Printed in Hungary

Correct citation
Pol, Floris van der and Suzanne Nederlof (eds). 2010. *Natural Resource Management in West Africa: Towards a knowledge management strategy.* Bulletin 392. Amsterdam, KIT Publishers

Keywords
Knowledge management, natural resource management, West Africa, rural development, social construction of knowledge

ISBN 978 94 6022 094-4
ISSN 0922-7911
NUR 600/940